A Must-Read Mexico Travel Guide For First Time Visiting

The Most Updated And Easy To Understand Guide On The Best Time And Places To Visit In Mexico, Trips To Oaxaca, Tulum Etc, Including Road Maps

By

Travel Guide Publishers

ABOUT THE PUBLISHERS

Travel Guide Publishers: Motivating Journeys, Informative Destinations

Travel Guide Publishers is a prominent distributing organization that has a practical understanding of making extraordinary travel guides for inquisitive explorers all around the planet. Enthusiastic about finding the unanticipated, yet critical fortunes and scandalous accomplishments of every side of the world, our organization endeavors to give extensive, trustworthy, and insightful resources for light craving for interest or experience and work with unprecedented journeys.

Spread out by a social occasion of enthusiastic travelers with an unquenchable craving for experience, Travel Guide Publishers comprehend the worth of changed and certifiable travel encounters.

With our far-reaching relationship with globetrotting well-informed authorities, we diligently curate spellbinding substance that solidifies a wide presentation of destinations, from clamoring metropolitan organizations to far-off wilds.

At Travel Guide Publishers, we recognize that traveling is an alternate choice from ticking off sights on an arrangement. It is associated with bringing down oneself in energetic social orders, banding together with neighborhood organizations, and expanding skylines. In that capacity, our travel guides go past the conventional thought of visiting to envelop and through data on history, culture, neighborhood customs, cooking, and past what might be for the most part expected attempts. We attempt to advance reasonable the travel business deals with, expecting to make a productive result for the two travelers and the spots they research.

Our serious social occasion of feature writers, visual subject matter experts, and editors work enthusiastically to make travel guides that are both staggering and well-off in data. We mix spellbinding visuals with drawing-in records to move readers to every destination, making the assessment cycle on a very basic level invigorating. Our far-reaching guides offer point-by-point plans, must-see attractions, down-to-earth tips, convenience thoughts, and insider snippets of data to enable travelers to take full advantage of their journeys.

With a substitute blend of travel guides covering different territories of land, nations, and metropolitan organizations, Travel Guide Publishers takes unprecedented thought of an assortment of traveler propensities. Whether you are a lot of experienced devotees, an outside voyager, or a food well-informed authority, our guides are fastidiously expected to manage various interests and travel styles.

In a period where improvement overwhelms the travel business, Travel Guide Publishers sees the significance of making with the times. We embrace electronic movements, offering our travel guides different courses of action, including modernized books, versatile applications, and insightful online stages. This guarantees that our guides are expeditiously available to present-day travelers, permitting them to convey the wellness of our travel area in their pockets.

Travel Guide Publishers has accumulated confidence in standing and a trustworthy readership because of our obligation to importance. We have been respected with respected grants for our extraordinary substance, plan, and commitment to the travel business. In any case, the authentic fulfillment lies in the positive examination we get from our readers, who keep on depending upon our guides for their travel attempts.

Whether you are setting out on a show researching experience, a family venture, or an over-the-top takeoff, Travel Guide Publishers is your confided sidekick. License us to be your guide as you track down the world, each spellbinding destination.

TABLE OF CONTENTS

INTRODUCTION

1.1 Outline of Mexico:

Mexico is a vibrant and diverse nation situated in North America, lined by the US toward the north and Guatemala and Belize toward the south. It is prestigious for its verifiable destinations, staggering sea shores, scrumptious cooking, and warm neighborliness. Mexico is the eleventh most crowded country on the planet and home to more than 130 million individuals.

1.2 History and Culture:

Mexico has a rich and interesting history that goes back millennia. The old civic establishments of the Maya, Aztecs, and Olmec lastingly affect the country. Demolishes like Chichen Itza, Teotihuacan, and Palenque draw in a large number of vacationers every year. The Spanish provincial time frame, which started in the sixteenth hundred years, carried a European impact on the nation's way of life, engineering, and language.

Mexican culture is known for its vibrant varieties, enthusiastic music, and conventional societal moves. The nation invests wholeheartedly in its imaginative expressions, including painting, figures, and writing. Mexican cooking is prestigious around the world, with dishes like tacos, enchiladas, and guacamole being staples. Try not to pass up on the potential chance to attempt legitimate Mexican road food during your visit.

1.3 Topography and Environment:

Mexico's geology is diverse, going from staggering shorelines to rough mountains and rambling deserts. The nation has a huge swath of scenes, including the Sierra Madre mountain goes, the Yucatan Promontory, and the Baja California Landmass.

Concerning the environment, Mexico encounters a scope of weather conditions because of its size and geology. As a general rule, the nation has heat and humidity, however unambiguous districts can have different weather patterns. The waterfront regions are ordinarily hot and sticky, making them ideal for ocean-side sweethearts. The focal high countries have a more mild environment, while northern Mexico can get very hot and dry. It's consistently really smart to take a look at the weather conditions conjecture for your particular objective before traveling.

1.4 When to Visit and Travel Fundamentals:

The best opportunity to visit Mexico relies upon the district you intend to investigate. As a general rule, the months between December and April are great for most regions, as they offer wonderful climates and fewer possibilities of downpours. Be that as it may, Mexico is an all-year objective, and each season has its appeal.

Travelers ought to pack in like manner for their Mexico trip. Here are a few fundamental things to consider:

- Lightweight and breathable apparel: Mexico's environment can be very hot, particularly in waterfront regions. Settle on light textures, for example, cotton or material to remain agreeable.

- Sun insurance: Remember to pack sunscreen, a wide-overflowed cap, and shades to safeguard yourself from the sun's beams.

- Bug repellent: Contingent upon your objective, you might experience mosquitoes or different bugs. It's really smart to convey bug repellent to stay away from any inconvenience.

- Agreeable footwear: Mexico's numerous attractions frequently require strolling or investigating by walking. Pack a couple of agreeable shoes or shoes for your touring undertakings.

- Travel reports: Guarantee you have a substantial identification with something like a half year of legitimacy remains. Furthermore, convey a printed or electronic duplicate of your travel schedule, lodging reservations, and some other fundamental records.

- Mexican pesos: While credit and charge cards are generally acknowledged, it's consistently useful to have some neighborhood money close by for little buys or on the off chance that you wind up in a spot that doesn't acknowledge cards.

Generally speaking, Mexico offers a diverse scope of encounters for travelers, from verifiable destinations to stunning regular miracles. By taking into account the nation's history, culture, geology, environment, and travel fundamentals, you can design a significant excursion to Mexico.

MAP OF MEXICO

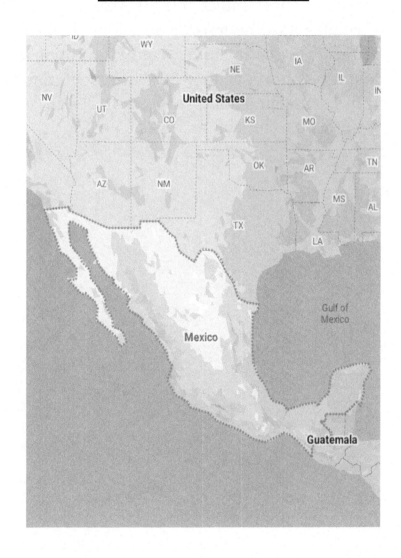

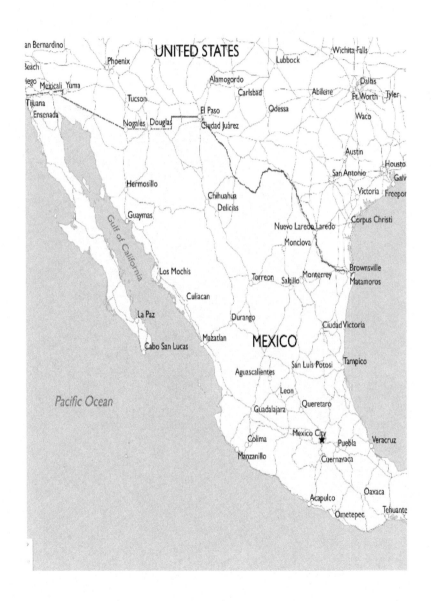

MAP OF MEXICO CITY

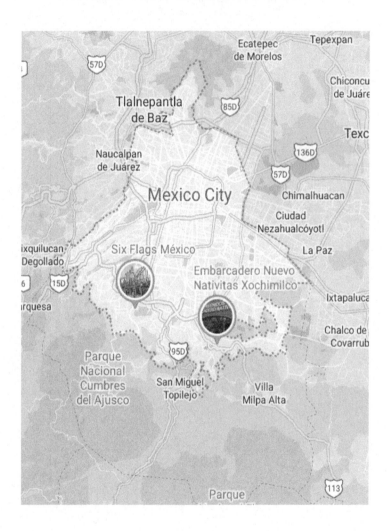

MAP OF OAXACA

ESSENTIAL MEXICO TRAVEL INFORMATION

2.1 Visa and Entry Requirements:

To enter Mexico, most foreign nationals require a valid passport. Depending on your nationality, you might have to obtain a visa before your trip or upon appearance. Guests from nations like the United States, Canada, the United Kingdom, Australia, and numerous European countries don't need a visa for the travel industry purposes and can remain for as long as 180 days. Be that as it may, it is constantly prescribed to check with the Mexican government office or department in your nation of origin for the most state-of-the-art information.

Visa and Entry Requirements for Mexico

Mexico is a well-known vacation location, and the visa and entry requirements for most nations are moderately direct. Be that as it may, it is essential to check the most recent requirements before you travel, as they can change every once in a while.

Who Needs a Mexico Visa?

Residents of most nations needn't bother with a visa to enter Mexico for the travel industry or business purposes for as long as 180 days. Be that as it may, there are a few special cases, including residents of Afghanistan, Bangladesh, Cuba, Iran, Iraq, North Korea, Pakistan, Somalia, Sudan, Syria, and Yemen. These nationals should obtain a visa before entering Mexico.

The most effective method to Apply for a Mexico Visa

On the off chance that you want a visa to enter Mexico, you can apply at the closest Mexican international haven or department. The application cycle ordinarily requires half a month, so it is essential to apply well ahead of your travel date.

What Documents Do You Want for a Mexico Visa?

The documents you want to apply for a Mexico visa will fluctuate depending on your nationality. Be that as it may, you will ordinarily have to give the accompanying:

A valid passport
A finished visa application form
A new passport-style photo
Verification of monetary help
Confirmation of forward travel
Entry Requirements for Mexico

Notwithstanding a visa, you will likewise have to meet the accompanying entry requirements for Mexico:

A valid passport with something like a half-year of validity

A finished Multiple Migratory Form (FMM)
Confirmation of forward travel
The Multiple Migratory Form (FMM)

The FMM is a report that all guests to Mexico should finish upon appearance. You can obtain the FMM at the air terminal or boundary crossing when you enter Mexico. The FMM is valid for as long as 180 days, and you should give up it when you leave Mexico.

Visa and Entry Requirements for Minors

On the off chance that you are traveling to Mexico with a minor, you should give extra documentation. This documentation might include:

The minor's birth certificate
The parent's or alternately gatekeeper's passport
A letter of consent from the other parent or gatekeeper, if pertinent.

Some more information on the visa and entry requirements for Mexico:

Visa exception: Residents of 69 nations are excluded from obtaining a visa to enter Mexico for the travel industry or business purposes for as long as 180 days. These nations incorporate the United States, Canada, most European nations, Australia, New Zealand, and Japan.

Visa application: On the off chance that you want a visa to enter Mexico, you can apply at the closest Mexican international haven or department. The application cycle ordinarily requires half a month, so it is essential to apply well ahead of your travel date.

You should give the accompanying documents when you apply for a visa:
A valid passport
A finished visa application form
A new passport-style photo

Verification of monetary help
Confirmation of forward travel

Multiple Migratory Form (FMM): All guests to Mexico should finish the Multiple Migratory Form (FMM) upon appearance. You can obtain the FMM at the air terminal or boundary crossing when you enter Mexico. The FMM is valid for as long as 180 days, and you should give up it when you leave Mexico.

Confirmation of forward travel: You should give verification of ahead travel when you enter Mexico. This could be a duplicate of your carrier ticket, a transport ticket, or a ship ticket.

Visa and entry requirements for minors: On the off chance that you are traveling to Mexico with a minor, you should give extra documentation. This documentation might include:
The minor's birth certificate

The parent's or alternately gatekeeper's passport

A letter of consent from the other parent or gatekeeper, if pertinent

I trust this makes a difference! On the off chance that you have some other inquiries, if it's not too much trouble, let me know.

End

The visa and entry requirements for Mexico are moderately direct for most nations. Be that as it may, it is essential to check the most recent requirements before you travel, as they can change every once in a while. You can track down the most recent information on the site of the Mexican government.

2.2 Currency and Cash Matters:

The authority currency of Mexico is the Mexican Peso (MXN). It is fitting to convey cash in more modest categories, as certain spots may not acknowledge enormous bills.

ATMs are generally accessible all through the nation, making it advantageous to pull out cash. Charge cards are additionally generally acknowledged in most vacationer regions, lodgings, and eateries. Be that as it may, it is prescribed to inform your bank or Mastercard organization about your travel intends to keep away from any issues with card utilization.

Here is some information about currency and cash matters in Mexico that you might view as valuable for your impending trip:

The authority currency of Mexico is the Mexican peso (MXN). The image for the peso is MXN, and it is frequently composed as MX to recognize it from different monetary standards that utilize the $ sign. The peso is partitioned into 100 centavos, however, centavos are seldom utilized in ordinary exchanges.

You can trade your currency for pesos at banks, currency trade authorities, and a few lodgings. The best trade rates are generally found at banks, however, they might be shut at the end of the week. Currency trade departments are much of the time open on the ends of the week, however, they might charge higher expenses.

You can likewise utilize your credit or charge card to pull out pesos from ATMs in Mexico. Notwithstanding, know that your bank might charge a foreign exchange expense.

On the off chance that you are anticipating utilizing your credit or charge card in Mexico, it is really smart to tell your bank ahead of time. This will assist with keeping your card from being declined because of misrepresentation counteraction measures.

Here are a few ways to involve cash in Mexico:

Continuously decide to be charged in pesos while utilizing your credit or check card. This will guarantee that you get the best conversion standard.

Know about the powerful currency transformation (DCC) choice while involving an ATM in Mexico. DCC permits you to be charged in your home currency, however, the conversion standard is generally more regrettable than if you are charged in pesos.

On the off chance that you are conveying cash, make certain to keep it in a protected spot. Unimportant burglary is an issue in Mexico, particularly in enormous urban communities.

Here are a few sites that can assist you with currency trade and cash matters in Mexico:

Some more information about currency and cash matters in Mexico:

The ongoing conversion standard for the Mexican peso is roughly USD 1 = 20 MXN. This conversion standard can vacillate, so it is consistently really smart to check the most recent rates before you travel.

At the point when you are trading your currency for pesos, it is essential to get the most ideal conversion standard. You can do this by contrasting rates at various banks and currency trade departments.

If you are utilizing your credit or charge card in Mexico, make certain to check with your bank to check whether there are any foreign exchange expenses. These expenses can fluctuate from one bank to another, so it is essential to know about them before you utilize your card.

On the off chance that you are conveying cash, make certain to keep it in a protected spot. Unimportant burglary is an issue in Mexico, so it is essential to be circumspect while conveying cash.

On the off chance that you are traveling to a distant area of Mexico, it is really smart to bring a few US dollars along with pesos. This is because a few organizations in distant regions may not acknowledge pesos.

Here are a few extra ways to involve cash in Mexico:

At the point when you are paying for something, consistently request the complete in pesos before you hand over your cash. This will assist with keeping you from being cheated.

On the off chance that you are shopping at a market, make certain to wrangle over costs. This is a typical practice in Mexico, and you can frequently get a more ideal arrangement by wheeling and dealing.

On the off chance that you are tipping, tipping in pesos is standard. The standard tip is 10% of the bill.

I trust this extra information is useful!

Some more information about currency and cash matters in Mexico:

Banks: Banks in Mexico are generally open from 9 am to 5 pm, Monday to Friday. A few banks may likewise be open on Saturdays.

Currency trade departments: Currency trade authorities are much of the time open longer hours than banks, and they might be open at the ends of the week. Be that as it may, they might charge higher expenses than banks.

ATMs: ATMs are generally accessible in Mexico, and they are much of the time situated in banks, shopping centers, and vacationer regions.

Credit and charge cards: Most credit and charge cards are acknowledged in Mexico, however, make certain to check with your bank to check whether there are any foreign exchange expenses.

Cash: It is really smart to convey money with you when you travel to Mexico, particularly on the off chance that you are traveling to a far-off region.

Wellbeing: Unimportant burglary is an issue in Mexico, so it is essential to be circumspect while conveying cash. It is likewise really smart to keep your cash in a protected spot, for example, a cash belt or a secret pocket.

Here are a few extra ways to involve cash in Mexico:

Do all necessary investigation: Before you travel, make certain to explore the ongoing conversion standard and the expenses related to utilizing your credit or charge card in Mexico.

Know about your environmental elements: When you are utilizing cash, make certain to know about your environmental elements and try not to pull out cash in jam-packed regions.

Use ATMs inside banks: ATMs situated inside banks are for the most part safer than ATMs situated in broad daylight places.

Report any lost or taken cards: On the off chance that you lose or have your credit or charge card taken, make certain to promptly report it to your bank.

I trust this extra information is useful!

2.3 Communication and Web Access:
Reaching out to your friends and family or getting to the web in Mexico is moderately simple. Mexico has an advanced telecommunication organization, and you can find various mobile organization suppliers offering paid ahead-of-time SIM cards for vacationers. Most significant urban communities and vacation locations have magnificent inclusion, however, know that far-off regions might have restricted or no sign.

Wi-Fi is typically accessible in lodgings, bistros, eateries, and air terminals. Be that as it may, it is consistently really smart to have a contingency plan, for example, buying a neighborhood SIM card for web access.

Mobile Telephones

Mobile telephones are the most well-known method for remaining associated in Mexico. There are three significant mobile telephone suppliers in Mexico.

You can purchase a paid ahead-of-time SIM card from any of the significant suppliers. These SIM cards are entirely reasonable, and they for the most part accompanied a couple of gigabytes of information. You can likewise purchase a month-to-month plan from a supplier, however, this is generally more costly.

Wi-Fi

Wi-Fi is generally accessible in Mexico, particularly in significant urban communities and vacation locations. You can track down Wi-Fi in lodgings, eateries, bistros, and, surprisingly, a few public spots.

The nature of Wi-Fi in Mexico can fluctuate. In certain spots, the Wi-Fi is quick and dependable. In different spots, the Wi-Fi is slow or untrustworthy. It's consistently really smart to have a contingency plan, like a mobile area of interest or a paid ahead-of-time SIM card with information.

Web Bistros

On the off chance that you want to involve the web where there is no Wi-Fi, you can go to a web bistro. Web bistros are normal in Mexico, and they are typically entirely reasonable.

Web Access in Provincial Regions

Web access in provincial areas of Mexico can be more restricted. In certain areas, there is no Wi-Fi or web bistros. If you are venturing out to a provincial region, it's really smart to check the web access choices before you go.

How Individuals Utilize the Web in Mexico

The web is utilized for different purposes in Mexico. The most widely recognized utilizes are:

Speaking with loved ones
Looking for data
Utilizing web-based entertainment
Shopping
Banking
Watching recordings
Messing around
Ways to Remain Associated in Mexico

The following are a couple of ways to remain associated in Mexico:

Purchase a paid ahead-of-time SIM card from a significant supplier.

Check the web access choices before you go to a provincial region.
Utilize a mobile area of interest or a paid ahead-of-time SIM card with information as a contingency plan.
Know about the security dangers of utilizing public Wi-Fi.
End

Communication and web access are not difficult to track down in Mexico. With just the right amount of arranging, you can remain associated all through your excursion.

Ways to remain Associated in Mexico:

Purchase a paid ahead-of-time SIM card from a significant supplier.
Check the web access choices before you go to a provincial region.
Utilize a mobile area of interest or a paid ahead-of-time SIM card with information as a contingency plan.

Know about the security dangers of utilizing public Wi-Fi.

Security Ways to Utilize Public Wi-Fi:

Try not to involve public Wi-Fi for delicate exercises, like banking or web-based shopping.

Utilize a VPN (virtual confidential organization) to scramble your traffic.

Know about the dangers of malware and phishing assaults.

Just associate with Wi-Fi networks that you trust.

I trust this data is useful. If it's not too much trouble, let me know whether you have some other inquiries.

2.4 Wellbeing and Security Tips:

Taking specific well-being and security precautionary measures while going to Mexico is significant. Here are a few hints to remember:

- Before making a trip to Mexico, it is prescribed to counsel your primary care physician or a movement wellbeing facility to guarantee you are state-of-the-art on routine immunizations and to ask about any extra immunizations or prescriptions you might require in light of your itinerary items.

- It is prudent to hydrate and try not to polish off regular water or ice that might have been produced using faucet water.

- Use sunscreen and wear defensive apparel, particularly in waterfront districts, as the sun can be very extraordinary.

- Mexico has gained notoriety for its fiery cooking, so on the off chance that you have a delicate stomach, settle on milder dishes or convey a prescription for stomach-related issues.

- Avoid potential risk against mosquito nibbles, particularly in districts where mosquito-borne sicknesses like dengue fever or Zika infection are predominant. Use bug repellent, wear long sleeves and jeans, and consider remaining in facilities with screens or cooling.

- Mexico is for the most part a protected country for explorers, however practicing watchfulness and practice presence of mind is consistently significant. Try not to show over-the-top abundance, be careful about pickpockets in jam-packed regions, and stick to sufficiently bright and populated places, particularly around evening time.

Wellbeing and Security Tips for First People who jump through time to Mexico

Mexico is a delightful country with a rich culture and history. It's likewise a well-known vacation location, with a large number of guests every year. Be that as it may, it's essential to know about the well-being and dangers before you travel to Mexico.

Here are some significant well-being and security tips for the first people who jump through time to Mexico:

Receive any available immunization shots. The Communities for Infectious Prevention and Counteraction (CDC) prescribes that all explorers to Mexico receive an immunization shot against hepatitis An and typhoid. You may likewise need to consider receiving any available immunization shots against yellow fever, contingent upon where you're visiting.

Hydrate. Try not to drink regular water in Mexico. It's undependable to drink, and it can make you debilitated. Filtered water is promptly accessible and reasonable, so there's not a glaringly obvious explanation to face the challenge.

Be cautious with road food. Road food is a scrumptious piece of Mexican culture, however, it's essential to be cautious while eating it. Ensure the food is prepared completely and that it's been taken care of cleanly.

Try not to swim in new water. Swimming in new water in Mexico can expand your gamble of getting a waterborne sickness. To swim, stick to saltwater sea shores.

Use bug repellent. Mosquitoes in Mexico can convey sicknesses like dengue fever and Zika infection. Use a bug repellent to safeguard yourself from mosquito nibbles.

Know about your environmental elements. Mexico is a protected nation, however, it's essential to know about your environmental elements, particularly around evening time. Try not to walk alone in disconnected regions, and don't streak your resources.

Remain informed. The U.S. Division of State has a tourism warning site that gives forward-thinking data on well-being and security in Mexico. Check the site before you travel to ensure you're mindful of any ongoing dangers.

By following these well-being and security tips, you can assist in guaranteeing that your excursion to Mexico is protected and agreeable.

Extra tips:

Pack an emergency treatment unit with fundamental supplies like swathes, anti-microbial salve, and painkillers.

On the off chance that you're making a trip to a distant region, think about bringing a satellite telephone or a different method for communication in the event of a crisis.

Gain proficiency with a few fundamental Spanish expressions before you go. This will assist you with speaking with local people and getting around more without any problems.

Be deferential to Mexican culture and customs. This will assist you with having a more certain and pleasant experience.

I trust these tips assist you with arranging a protected and pleasant excursion to Mexico!

2.5 Transportation in Mexico:
Mexico offers different methods of transportation to investigate the country:

- Homegrown Flights: Mexico has a very much associated homegrown flight organization, making it helpful to go between significant urban communities and vacationer locations.
- Transports: Mexico has a broad transport network that is reasonable and dependable. Transports range from extravagant mentors with conveniences like cooling and happy seating to more straightforward choices.
- Trains: While train travel isn't as predominant in Mexico as transports or flights, there are a couple of picturesque train courses, for example, the Copper Ravine train, which takes you through stunning scenes in the north of the country.

- Rental Vehicles: Leasing a vehicle can give adaptability, particularly on the off chance that you wish to investigate distant regions or go on travels. Notwithstanding, know that driving in enormous urban communities can be tumultuous, and it is essential to adhere to neighborhood traffic guidelines and guidelines.

- Taxis: Cabs are generally accessible in Mexico, however, it is prescribed to utilize approved taxis from assigned stands or request that your lodging call a respectable taxi administration. In bigger urban communities, administrations like booking carb are additionally accessible.

While utilizing public transportation or taxicabs, be mindful of your possessions and try not to show costly things to limit the gamble of burglary.

MEXICO CITY

3.1 Investigating the Historic Center:

Mexico City's Historic Center, otherwise called Centro Histórico, is a Essential World Legacy site and the core of the city. It is home to the absolute most significant historical and social destinations in Mexico. Investigating the Historic Center is an unquestionable requirement for any explorer visiting Mexico.

One of the fundamental attractions in the Historic Center is the Zócalo, otherwise called the Square de la Constitución. It is quite possibly the biggest square on the planet and is encircled by significant structures like the Metropolitan Church building, the Public Royal residence, and the Sanctuary City hall leader. The Zócalo is an energetic spot where local people and vacationers accumulate to unwind, appreciate road entertainers, and absorb the environment.

A feature of investigating the Historic Center is visiting the staggering Metropolitan Church building. Worked throughout almost three centuries, it is the biggest house of prayer in the Americas and a compositional show-stopper. Inside, guests can investigate its various houses of prayer and appreciate its delightful stained glass windows.

Another must-visit site is the Public Royal residence. This noteworthy structure houses the workplace of the Leader of Mexico and is additionally home to some of Diego Rivera's well-known wall paintings. These wall paintings portray significant occasions in Mexican history and are something truly amazing.

Notwithstanding these notorious destinations, the Historic Center is additionally home to various exhibition halls, shops, and eateries. Guests can investigate the Historical Center of Expressive Arts, which includes a broad assortment of Mexican and worldwide craftsmanship. They can likewise meander through the energetic roads of the Centro Histórico and visit neighborhood shops selling painstaking work and conventional Mexican items.

Mexico is a country with a rich and different history, and its historic centers are a demonstration of that. From the antiquated remnants of Teotihuacan to the provincial urban communities of Puebla and Morelia, there are endless spots to investigate in Mexico that will move you back in time.

For first-people who jump through time, it very well may be a piece overwhelming to know where to begin. Be that as it may, simply sit back and relax, I'm here to help. The following are a couple of the best historic centers in Mexico that are ideally suited for first-time guests:

Mexico City: The historic center of Mexico City is a Essential World Legacy Site and is home to probably the most notorious milestones in the nation, including the Zocalo, the Metropolitan House of Prayer, and the Templo Chairman. There are additionally endless historical centers, markets, and eateries to investigate in this energetic city.

Puebla: Puebla is a provincial city that is known for its wonderful engineering, including the St Nick Rosa Church and the Palacio del Gobierno. The city is likewise home to various significant historical locales, like the Pyramid of Cholula and the Ex-Convento de St Nick Monica.

Morelia: Morelia is one more provincial city that is known for its all-around safeguarded engineering. The city's fundamental square, the Court de Armas, is one of the most gorgeous in Mexico. There are likewise various historical centers and places of worship to investigate in Morelia, including the Catedral de Morelia and the Museo del Carmen.

Oaxaca: Oaxaca is a city that is wealthy in culture and history. The city's historic center is home to various significant milestones, including the Santo Domingo Church and the Monte Albán ruins. There are likewise various historical centers and markets to investigate in Oaxaca, making it an extraordinary spot to find out about the way of life of the district.

These are only a couple of the numerous extraordinary historic centers in Mexico. With such a great amount to see and do, you're certain to have a significant encounter regardless of where you go.

Here are some ways to design your excursion to a historic center in Mexico:

Begin by doing all necessary investigations. There are a ton of extraordinary historic centers in Mexico, so it's essential to do all necessary investigations and conclude which one is ideal for you. Consider your inclinations and what you're expecting to see and do.

Book your facilities early. The historic centers in Mexico are well-known vacation locations, so it's essential to book your facilities early, particularly on the off chance that you're going during the pinnacle season.

Plan your transportation. The historic centers in Mexico are frequently walkable, however, you might need to think about leasing a vehicle or taking public transportation on the off chance that you're anticipating visiting at least one or two spots.

Dress serenely. You'll do a great deal of strolling in the historic centers, so make a point to pack agreeable shoes and dress.

Be ready for swarms. The historic centers in Mexico can become busy, particularly during the pinnacle season. Be ready for long queues at well-known vacation destinations.

Be deferential to the neighborhood culture. While visiting a historic center in Mexico, it's essential to be deferential to the neighborhood culture. This implies dressing fittingly, keeping away from clear commotions, and being aware of your environmental elements.

Considering these tips, you're certain to live it up by investigating the historic centers in Mexico. So the thing would you say you are hanging tight for? Begin arranging your excursion today!

3.2 Historical Centers and Craftsmanship Exhibitions:

Mexico City is known for its rich social legacy and energetic craftsmanship scene. The city is home to various historical centers and craftsmanship exhibitions that grandstand both Mexican and worldwide workmanship.

Quite possibly of the most prestigious historical center in Mexico City is the Frida Kahlo Exhibition Hall, otherwise called the Blue House. Situated in the neighborhood of Coyoacán, it was the previous home of Frida

Kahlo and Diego Rivera. The historical center houses an assortment of Kahlo's compositions, individual possessions, and works by other Mexican specialists. It gives an interesting understanding of Kahlo's life and craftsmanship.

The Public Historical Center of Human Sciences is another must-visit exhibition hall in Mexico City. It is quite possibly the main archeological historical center on the planet and houses a tremendous assortment of relics from pre-Hispanic civic establishments. From the Aztecs to the Mayans, guests can investigate the rich history and culture of antiquated Mexico through its broad displays.

Craftsmanship sweethearts will likewise appreciate visiting the Soumaya Historical Center, which is home to one of the biggest assortments of workmanship in Latin America. The historical center grandstands a noteworthy scope of works, from old figures to contemporary craftsmanship. Its one-of-a-kind plan, with a well-proportioned silver outside, is likewise an incredible sight.

Notwithstanding these significant historical centers, Mexico City is spotted with craftsmanship exhibitions that grandstand crafted by both laid out and arising specialists. The energetic neighborhoods of Roma and Condesa are especially known for their specialty scenes, with various exhibitions and road craftsmanship show.

The followings are a couple of the best historical centers and craftsmanship exhibitions in Mexico for the first people who jump through time:

Museo Nacional de Antropología (Public Historical Center of Human Sciences) in Mexico City is one of the biggest and most far-reaching human sciences exhibition halls on the planet. It houses a broad assortment of curios from Mexico's pre-Hispanic societies, including the Aztecs, Maya, and Olmecs.

Museo Frida Kahlo (Frida Kahlo Historical Center) in Coyoacán, Mexico City is the previous home and studio of the well-known Mexican craftsman. The historical center is loaded up with Kahlo's compositions, individual possessions, and photos, offering an interesting look into her life and work.

Palacio de Bellas Artes (Royal Residence of Expressive Arts) in Mexico City is a staggering illustration of mid-twentieth-century engineering. The royal residence houses various craftsmanship exhibitions, as well as a theater and a drama house.

Museo Soumaya in Mexico City is a confidential historical center that houses an assortment of present-day and contemporary craftsmanship. The historical center's assortment incorporates works by Picasso, Dalí, and Van Gogh.

Museo Jumex in Mexico City is one more confidential historical center that houses an assortment of present-day and contemporary craftsmanship. The historical center's assortment incorporates works by Jeff Koons, Damien Hirst, and Andy Warhol.

Notwithstanding these significant historical centers, there are numerous more modest craftsmanship exhibitions and galleries to investigate in Mexico. If you're keen on contemporary craftsmanship, make certain to look at the workmanship scene in San Miguel de Allende. This enchanting provincial town is home to various exhibitions and studios that grandstand crafted by neighborhood and worldwide specialists.

Regardless of what your inclinations are, you're certain to track down something to see the value in Mexico's historical centers and craftsmanship exhibitions. So whenever you're arranging an excursion to Mexico, make certain to add a couple of these social establishments to your schedule.

Here are a few extra ways to visit historical centers and craftsmanship exhibitions in Mexico:

Numerous historical centers offer free or limited confirmation on specific days of the week, so make certain to check the exhibition hall's site before you go.
On the off chance that you're visiting a well-known historical center, be ready for swarms. Attempt to visit during the slow time of year or during the week to keep away from the greatest groups.

Numerous historical centers have sound aids accessible in different dialects. This is an extraordinary method for diving more deeply into the displays without perusing all of the wall text.

If you're keen on taking photographs, make certain to check the historical center's arrangement before you begin snapping pictures. A few historical centers have limitations on photography, particularly in the extraordinary displays.
I trust this makes a difference!

3.3. Chapultepec Park and Palace:

Chapultepec Park is a rambling green desert garden in the core of Mexico City. It is one of the largest city parks in the world, with more than 1,600 acres, and it is a popular place for locals and tourists to relax.

The recreation area is home to various attractions, including the notorious Chapultepec Palace. Roosted on a slope sitting above the recreation area, the palace offers stunning perspectives on Mexico City's horizon. It was once the residence of Mexican emperors and a military academy in the past. Today, it houses the Public Historical Center of History, where guests can investigate the rich history of Mexico through its great assortment of curios and displays.

Investigating Chapultepec Park itself is a brilliant encounter. It offers tranquil walking trails, boat rentals for lake paddling, and picnicking under ancient trees for visitors. The Chapultepec Zoo, one of Latin America's oldest and most significant zoos, is also located in the park. It has educational programs and exhibits, houses a wide range of animal species, and is located there.

The Modern Art Museum housed within an exquisite Art Deco building, is yet another feature of Chapultepec Park that deserves to be noted. From the 20th century to the present, works by Mexican artists are on display at the museum. It has paintings, sculptures, and installations in its collection that show the creativity and variety of Mexican contemporary art.

Chapultepec Park is one of the most well-known traveler objections in Mexico City. It is a tremendous, 686-hectare (1,695-section of land) park situated in the core of the city, and it is home to a wide assortment of attractions, including Chapultepec Palace, the Public Exhibition Hall of Human Sciences, the Chapultepec Zoo, and the Chapultepec Palace Public History Gallery.

Chapultepec Palace is the most notable milestone in the recreation area. In the 18th century, it was constructed as a summer palace for the Spanish viceroys. Later, it was used as the residence of Empress Carlota and Emperor Maximilian. The castle is now a museum that displays Mexican and European artifacts and art.

One of Mexico's most important and largest museums is the National Museum of Anthropology. It houses an immense assortment of curios from everywhere in the nation, including pre-Columbian models, materials, and gems. Anyone who wants to learn more about the fascinating history and culture of Mexico should go to the museum.

The Chapultepec Zoo is one of the most established and famous zoos in Mexico. It is home to north of 2,000 creatures from around the world, including lions, tigers, bears, and giraffes. The zoo is a great place to spend the day outdoors and learn about animals.

Notwithstanding these significant attractions, Chapultepec Park likewise has various things to see and do. There are gardens, lakes, wellsprings, and various strolling and trekking trails. Additionally, the park is a popular location for picnics, events, and concerts.

The beautiful and lively Chapultepec Park has something for everyone. Chapultepec Park is a great place to go if you want to learn about history, culture, and nature, or just spend the day enjoying the great outdoors.

The following are some additional hints for touring Chapultepec Castle and Park:

Every day, the park is open from 6 a.m. to 6 p.m.
The National History Museum and the castle both cost 85 pesos, or $4.25, to enter.
The park has several cafes and restaurants, but you can also bring your food and beverages.
The recreation area can become busy, particularly at the end of the week, so it is ideal to early show up.

Because there is a lot of walking involved, you should bring comfortable shoes if you plan to visit the castle.

Certainly, here is some more data about Chapultepec Park and Palace:

Chapultepec Palace is a wonderful illustration of Neoclassical and Gothic Recovery engineering. It is on top of Chapultepec Hill, and from there, you can see the entire city. The castle has served as a summer palace for the Spanish viceroys, a military academy, and the official residence of Emperor Maximilian and Empress Carlota throughout its history. The castle is now a museum that displays Mexican and European artifacts and art.

The Public Historical Center of Human Sciences is one of the biggest and most significant exhibition halls in Mexico. It is home to a sizable collection of artifacts from all over the nation, including jewelry, textiles, and pre-Columbian sculptures. The gallery is separated into a few segments, every one of which is devoted to an alternate time in Mexican history.

The Chapultepec Zoo is one of the most seasoned and well-known zoos in Mexico. It is home to north of 2,000 creatures from around the world, including lions, tigers, bears, and giraffes. The zoo is separated into a few segments, every one of which is devoted to an alternate mainland.

Notwithstanding these significant attractions, Chapultepec Park likewise has various things to see and do. There are gardens, lakes, wellsprings, and various strolling and trekking trails. Additionally, the park is a popular location for picnics, events, and concerts.

The following are some additional hints for touring Chapultepec Castle and Park:

Visit the National Museum of Anthropology and the castle if you are interested in history.
Assuming you are keen on creatures, make certain to visit the Chapultepec Zoo.

Make sure to visit one of the park's numerous gardens or lakes if you want to unwind.

If you are visiting during the end of the week, make certain to show up before the expected time as the recreation area can become busy.

I hope this helps you prepare for your trip to Chapultepec Castle and Park!

3.4 Mexico City Day Trips:

In addition to Mexico City's numerous tourist attractions, several fantastic day trips can be taken within a short distance. These road trips offer an opportunity to investigate a greater amount of Mexico's rich culture, history, and regular scenes.

One of Mexico City's most popular day trips is to Teotihuacan. Found only 30 miles upper east of the city, this antiquated

Mesoamerican city is home to the renowned Pyramid of the Sun and Pyramid of the Moon. Guests can climb these pyramids to respect all-encompassing perspectives on the encompassing remnants and wonder about the engineering marvels of the pre-Columbian time.

Another incredible road trip choice is to visit the beguiling town of Puebla. Found southeast of Mexico City, Puebla is known for its staggering frontier design and its scrumptious cooking. The notable focus of Puebla is a Essential World Legacy site and highlights wonderful temples, energetic courts, and perfectly tiled structures. Guests can investigate the city's rich history and enjoy its well-known culinary pleasures, for example, mole poblano and chiles en nogada.

A day trip to the Monarch Butterfly Biosphere Reserve is a must for nature lovers. Found a couple of hours west of

Mexico City, this hold is a Essential World Legacy site and fills in as a haven for a large number of ruler butterflies. During the monarch migration season (November to March), visitors can hike through the pine forests of the reserve to see the incredible movement of millions of butterflies.

Mexico City is a sprawling metropolis with a lot to see and do, but you can also take a lot of fun day trips from the city. A few of the best are as follows:

Teotihuacan: With good reason, this ancient city is one of Mexico's most popular tourist destinations. The Pyramid of the Sun and the Pyramid of the Moon are two of the most noteworthy pyramids on the planet, and the site is likewise home to various sanctuaries, castles, and pyramids.

Xochimilco: Experience traditional Mexican culture at this floating garden, a Essential World Heritage Site. You can go to one of the many markets or restaurants or rent a trajinera, or a colorful boat, and take a leisurely cruise through the canals.

Puebla: This colonial city is well-known for its stunning architecture, mouthwatering cuisine, and lively culture. The cathedral is a Essential World Heritage Site, and the Zócalo, the city's main square, is one of the largest in Latin America.

Cholula: This city is home to the Incomparable Pyramid of Cholula, which is the biggest pyramid on the planet by volume. The pyramid is a shortened mountain that has been developed after some time, and it is topped by a congregation.

Taxco: This city is known for its silver mines and its silver gems. The city's fundamental square, the Court Borda, is fixed with shops selling silver gems, and there are likewise various silver galleries in the city.

These are only a couple of the numerous extraordinary road trips that can be delighted in from Mexico City. With such countless choices to browse, you're certain to find the ideal road trip to accommodate your inclinations.

Additional pointers for arranging day trips from Mexico City include the following:

Book your visits ahead of time: This is especially crucial for well-known locations like Puebla and Teotihuacan.

Take public transportation: This is a fantastic way to save money and learn about the culture of the area.

Bring water, sunscreen, and a hat: It's important to be prepared for Mexico City's hot and sunny weather.

Get up early: You'll have more time to explore and avoid the crowds thanks to this.

I trust this makes a difference!

Teotihuacan

Cholula

Taxco

Other day trips from Mexico City include the following:

Tepoztlán: This charming mountain town is well-known for its enchanting scenery, ancient pyramids, and ethereal energy. You can climb to the highest point of the Tepozteco Pyramid, visit the vestiges of the antiquated city of Xochicalco, or essentially loosen up in the town's numerous spas.

The Val de Bravo: The mountains surrounding this picturesque lakeside town make it a popular spot for boating, fishing, and hiking. You can likewise visit the town's numerous cascades, or require a road trip to the close by town of Avándaro.

Cacahuamilpa Grutas: Numerous stalactites and stalagmites can be found in these stunning caves in the state of Guerrero. The caves can be explored on your own or with a tour guide.

The Stands: On a hot day, this natural water park in the state of Morelos is a great place to cool off. You can swim in the recreation area's many pools, go tubing down the stream, or take a stab at bluff hopping.

Sanctuary for Monarch Butterflies: This asylum is situated in the territory of Michoacán and is home to a large number of ruler butterflies. You can visit the haven throughout the cold weather for a long time to see the butterflies right at home.

I trust this gives you much more choices to browse while arranging your road trip from Mexico City. Enjoy!

All in all, Mexico City offers plenty of attractions and encounters for explorers. This vibrant and culturally diverse city has something for everyone, from exploring the historic center and its iconic landmarks to learning about art and visiting the stunning Chapultepec Park and Castle. In addition, visitors can further immerse themselves in Mexico's history, natural beauty, and customs by taking advantage of the fantastic day trips available in the region.

CANCUN AND THE RIVIERA MAYA

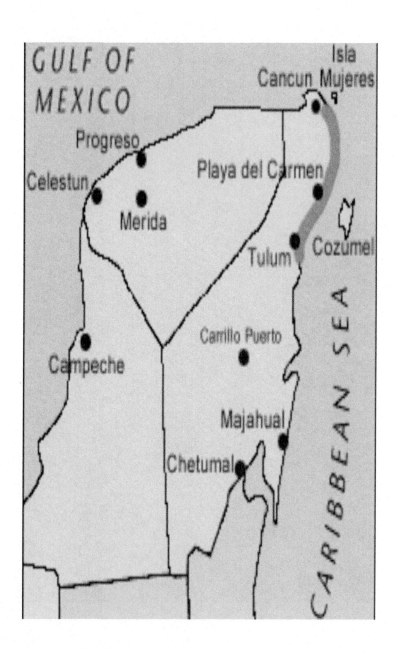

Cancun and the Riviera Maya, situated along Mexico's shocking Caribbean shore, offer a variety of extraordinary encounters that take special care of every explorer's longings.

4.1 Cancun's Beaches and Resorts:
Cancun, eminent for its flawless white sand sea shores and completely clear turquoise waters, is a heaven for ocean-side sweethearts. You can't help but feel a sense of peace wash over you as the sun rises above the horizon and shines golden on the sandy shore. The seashores here, like Playa Delfines and Playa Tortugas, gloat stunning excellence and give the ideal setting for sunbathing, swimming, or lolling in the warm tropical mood. Numerous opulent resorts rise majestically along the coastline, providing world-class amenities, delectable cuisine, and unparalleled hospitality. Whether you look for a comprehensive safe house or a shop hideout, Cancun's retreats

take special care of every taste, guaranteeing that your visit is loaded up with unwinding and guilty pleasures.

Cancun has miles of white-sand beaches, crystal-clear waters, and stunning coral reefs, making it a popular beach destination worldwide. The seashores in Cancun are probably the most incredible on the planet, and they offer something for everybody, from swimming and sunbathing to swimming and plunging.

There are two main areas of Cancun's beaches: both the North and South Zones. Playa Norte, Playa Maroma, and Playa Delfines are among Cancun's most popular beaches in the North Zone. The soft sand, calm waters, and stunning views that these beaches offer are well-known. Playa Chac Mool and Playa Punta Nizuc are two of Cancun's more remote beaches that are located in the South Zone. These sea shores are ideally suited for people who need to get

87

away from the groups and loosen up in harmony.

Cancun offers a wide selection of resorts in addition to its beaches. From luxury all-inclusive resorts to budget-friendly beachfront hotels, there are resorts to suit every budget and taste.

Cancun's best beaches and resorts are as follows:

Playa Norte Beach: This is perhaps of the most famous ocean side in Cancun, and seeing why is simple. The water is calm and clear, the sand is soft, and the views of the Caribbean Sea are breathtaking.

Maroma Strand: The smooth, white sand and calm, clear waters of this beach are well-known. You can swim, sunbathe, and unwind here.

The Delfines Playa This ocean side is situated toward the finish of the Cancun Inn Zone, and it's an incredible spot to take a dip, sunbathe, or go swimming or jumping.

Playa Chac Mool: This beach in the South Zone of Cancun is great for swimming, sunbathing, and exploring the Mayan ruins nearby.

Punta Nizuc Playa: This beach is great for swimming, sunbathing, snorkeling, and diving. It is in the South Zone of Cancun.

Cancun's Le Blanc Spa Resort: On Playa Norte, this luxurious resort has stunning views of the Caribbean Sea. There are five restaurants, a spa, and a fitness center at the resort.

Hyatt Ziva Cancun: On Playa del Carmen, this all-inclusive resort offers a wide range of activities, including swimming, sunbathing, snorkeling, scuba diving, and water sports.

Moon Castle Cancun: On the Riviera Maya, this all-inclusive resort offers a wide range of activities, including swimming, sunbathing, snorkeling, diving, and water sports.

Cancun's Live Aqua Beach Resort: This everything comprehensive retreat is situated in Playa del Carmen, and it offers various exercises, including swimming, sunbathing, swimming, jumping, and water sports.

The Vine Cancun's Secrets: On Playa del Carmen, this all-inclusive resort for adults only offers a wide range of activities, such as swimming, sunbathing, snorkeling, diving, and water sports.

Whether you're searching for a loosening up ocean-side excursion or an activity-stuffed experience, Cancun has something for everybody. Cancun is the ideal location to get away from the every day and make memories that will last a lifetime thanks to its breathtaking beaches, crystal-clear waters, and world-class resorts.

4.2 Exploring the Mayan Sites of Tulum:
The captivating town of Tulum is just a short drive from Cancun and is home to the remains of an ancient civilization that once thrived in this coastal paradise. The energy of a bygone era permeates the air as soon as you enter the Mayan ruins in Tulum. The stone designs, outlined against a setting of turquoise waters, stand as a demonstration of the immortal splendor of Mayan engineering. Go for a relaxed walk along the raised pathways, envisioning the day-to-day routines once experienced inside these striking walls. Awe ishes over you as you approach the cliffside Castillo and take in the breathtaking view of the Caribbean Sea stretching into infinity. The ruins of Tulum

provide a window into the past, blending history and natural beauty seamlessly.

On the Mexican Caribbean coast, Tulum is a beautiful town with some of the country's most impressive Mayan ruins. The Tulum Archaeological Site is on a cliff with a view of the sea. From here, you can see the coast and the jungle all around.

The Mayans constructed the ruins in the 13th century when they were a significant trading port. El Castillo, a massive 40-meter-tall pyramid, is one of the impressive structures on the site, which is well preserved.

The Tulum Archaeological Site has a lot to offer visitors in terms of sights and activities. You can investigate the vestiges, climb El Castillo, and visit the Sanctuary of the Frescoes, which is enhanced with lovely wall paintings. Additionally, you can stroll the beach, swim in the water, or go snorkeling or diving in the nearby reefs.

Because the Tulum Archaeological Site is a popular tourist destination, it is best to visit in the early morning or late afternoon to avoid crowds. Because the ruins can be hot and sunny, you should also bring a hat, sunscreen, and comfortable shoes.

The Mayan ruins of Tulum can be explored in a few different ways:

Show up before the expected time in the first part of the day to beat the groups.
Wear agreeable shoes, sunscreen, and a cap.
Bring a water container and bites.
Take as much time as necessary to investigate the remnants and absorb the environment.
For magnificent views of the coastline, don't forget to climb El Castillo.
Beautiful Mayan murals can be seen when you go to the Temple of the Frescoes.

Go swimming in the ocean or taking a stroll along the beach.

Scuba dive or snorkel among the nearby reefs.

The Mayan ruins of Tulum are a truly unforgettable experience. The Mayan people's ingenuity and creativity are evident in the ruins, which also provide an intriguing window into the past. If you're arranging an excursion to Mexico, make certain to add the Tulum Archeological Site to your schedule.

For those planning a trip to the Tulum Archaeological Site, here are some additional travel tips:

The extra charge is 75 pesos for grown-ups and 25 pesos for kids.

Seven days a week, the ruin is open from 8:00 a.m. to 5:00 p.m.

At the entrance to the ruins, there is a parking lot, but it can get crowded.

The ruins can be visited on guided tours by a variety of tour companies.
The ruins can also be explored on your own.

I trust this makes a difference!

4.3 Cozumel Scuba Diving and Snorkeling:
With its unrivaled underwater world, Cozumel, a lively island off the coast of the Riviera Maya, draws adventure seekers. Lash on your snorkel stuff or scuba jumping gear and submerge yourself in the entrancing coral reefs abounding with beautiful marine life. The completely clear waters of Cozumel uncover a universe of marvel and stunningness, as huge coral developments make a permanent place to stay for incalculable exotic fish, lively ocean turtles, and, surprisingly, smooth stingrays. Plunge profoundly into the profundities, investigating submerged caverns and gullies, or float easily on a superficial level, hypnotized by the kaleidoscope of varieties that encompass you. The underwater

playground of Cozumel offers an unforgettable experience.

Cozumel is an incredibly famous scuba plunging and swimming objective and for good explanation. The unmistakable, turquoise waters off the shore of Cozumel are home to an inconceivable assortment of marine life, including coral reefs, fish, turtles, and beams.

The following are some of Cozumel's best snorkeling and diving spots:

Reef Palancar: This is one of the most well-known swimming and jumping spots in Cozumel and is for good explanation. The reef is home to a wide assortment of marine life, including bright coral, ocean turtles, and fish.

Columbia's Submerged Reef: This reef is found simply off the shore of Cozumel, and it's an extraordinary spot for swimmers, everything being equal. The shallow water makes it simple to see the coral and fish, and there are a lot of chances to swim with ocean turtles.

The Light: The incredible visibility of this reef, which can be found in the southern part of Cozumel, is well-known. The water is obvious to such an extent that you can see up to 100 feet beneath the surface, and the reef is home to a wide assortment of marine life, including sharks, beams, and dolphins.

Reef of Chankanaab: In the Chankanaab National Marine Park, this reef is a great spot for divers and snorkelers of all levels. The recreation area has different swimming and plunging trails, and there are likewise potential chances to swim with dolphins and ocean turtles.

Wall of Santa Rosa: South of Cozumel, this wall is a great spot for experienced divers and snorkelers. The wall drops off to a profundity of more than 1,000 feet, and it's home to an assortment of marine life, including sharks, beams, and fish.

In Cozumel, you'll have a great time snorkeling or diving, no matter how experienced you are. Cozumel is a diver's paradise due to its crystal-clear waters, stunning coral reefs, and abundance of marine life.

When you should go: During the dry season, which lasts from May to September, is the best time to go snorkeling and diving in Cozumel. The weather is warm and sunny at this time, and the water is clear and calm.

How to reach it: Cozumel is off the coast of the Yucatán Peninsula in Mexico. You can take a ferry from Playa del Carmen or fly to the International Airport of Cozumel.

Stay where: There are different lodgings and resorts in Cozumel that take care of swimmers and jumpers. The following are some of the best-rated hotels for snorkeling and diving:

Cozumel's Live Aqua Beach Resort: This hotel has a confidential ocean side, a dip-up bar, and various swimming and plunging bundles.

The Cozumel Palace Hotel: There is a lazy river, a water park, and a variety of snorkeling and diving excursions at this resort.

Ziva Hyatt: Cozumel: This resort offers snorkeling and diving packages as well as a kids' club and swim-up bar.

What to pack: Make sure to bring the following items with you when packing for your trip to Cozumel to snorkel or dive:

Swim gear: This incorporates a cover, snorkel, blades, and a rash gatekeeper.

Diver's gear: A weight belt, a wetsuit, a mask, a snorkel, fins, a regulator, a buoyancy compensator, and a mask are all items you'll need for scuba diving.

Shade from the sun: This incorporates sunscreen, a cap, and shades.

Waterproof camera: You will be able to record your underwater adventures in this way.

Tips:

Book your swimming or plunging visit ahead of time: Especially during the peak season, this is crucial.

Check the weather forecast carefully: You might want to change the date of your trip if it looks like it will rain.

Pay attention to your aide: They can assist you in remaining safe and getting the most out of your underwater experience.

Have a ball! Scuba diving and snorkeling in Cozumel are unforgettable experiences.

The Riviera Maya's ecotourism:
The Riviera Maya has many ecotourism activities for people who want to get closer to nature. Enjoy thrilling zipline adventures that take you through the treetops and offer panoramic views of the lush landscape as you travel through the jungle. An ethereal world of stalactites and subterranean rivers awaits in vast underground cenotes, sacred sinkholes formed by collapsed limestone caverns. As you paddle through the tranquil waters of the Sian Ka'an Biosphere Reserve, which is home to numerous bird species, crocodiles, and even jaguars, embark on a wildlife encounter. Ecotourism activities in the Riviera Maya are not only exhilarating but also sustainable, allowing you to fully immerse yourself in this one-of-a-kind ecosystem with no worries about the environment.

The Riviera Maya is a lovely district of Mexico that is home to an abundance of regular excellence and social legacy. It is also a popular ecotourism destination where visitors can see the unique ecosystems of the area and learn about its long history.

The absolute most famous ecotourism exercises in the Riviera Maya include:

Diving and snorkeling: Some of the best snorkeling and diving in the world can be found in the Riviera Maya. Guests can investigate the clear waters of the Caribbean Ocean, where they can see an assortment of beautiful fish, coral reefs, and even wrecks.

Visiting cenotes: Natural sinkholes known as cenotes can be found all over the Yucatán Peninsula. They are frequently loaded up with completely clear water, making them ideal for swimming, swimming, and jumping. The Mayan people regard cenotes as sacred as well, and many of them are still used for religious ceremonies.

Bicycles and hiking: Numerous biking and hiking trails wind through lush jungles and along stunning beaches in the Riviera Maya. Visitors can take in the diverse ecosystems and wildlife of the area on these trails.

Visiting Mayan ruins: Numerous ancient Mayan ruins, including Chichen Itza, Tulum, and Coba, can be found on the Riviera Maya. These vestiges offer guests a brief look into the rich history and culture of the Mayan public.

Learning about the ancient culture of the Maya: There are various chances to find out about conventional Mayan culture in the Riviera Maya. Participants can take part in customary ceremonies, see Mayan villages, and learn about Mayan cooking.

Ecotourism is a great way to see the natural beauty and cultural heritage of the Riviera Maya while also helping to protect the environment. By participating in ecotourism activities, you are supporting businesses that are committed to environmentally friendly practices.

Here are a few ways to design an ecotourism outing to the Riviera Maya:

Do your homework: The Riviera Maya is home to a plethora of ecotourism operators. Find one that is committed to environmentally friendly practices by conducting research.

Select activities that won't have a big impact: Choose ecotourism activities that don't have a lot of negative effects on the environment. This could incorporate exercises like climbing, trekking, and visiting cenotes.

Give back to local businesses: When you're in the Riviera Maya, help the local businesses that are dedicated to using environmentally friendly methods. This will assist with guaranteeing that your cash is returning to the local area.

Be considerate of the surroundings: Respect the environment whenever you participate in ecotourism activities. This means respecting wildlife, leaving no trace, and adhering to your tour operator's guidelines.

Ecotourism is a great way to see the Riviera Maya and help preserve the environment at the same time. By following these tips, you can guarantee that your excursion is both agreeable and maintainable.

All in all, Cancun and the Riviera Maya offer a gold mine of encounters that take special care of every sort of explorer. This travel guide provides a glimpse into the wonders that Mexico's Caribbean coast has to offer, including idyllic beaches and opulent resorts, ancient ruins, and captivating underwater worlds. So gather your sacks, set foot on this sun-kissed heaven, and let the wizardry of Cancun and the Riviera Maya unfurl right in front of you.

GUADALAJARA AND THE
WESTERN REGION

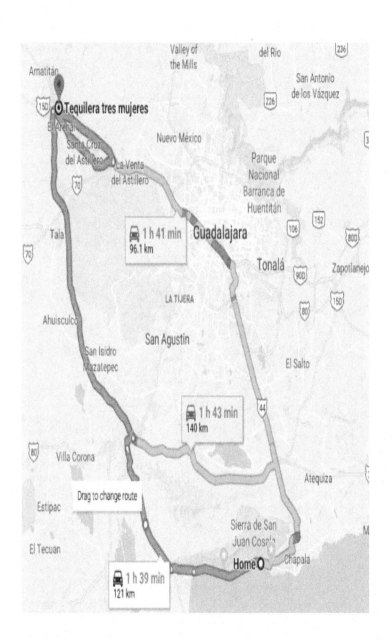

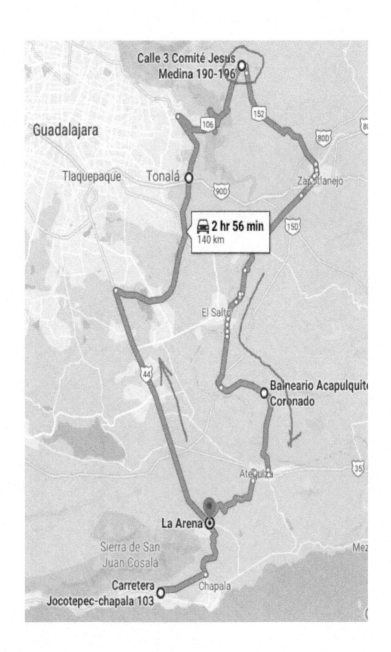

The state capital of Jalisco is Guadalajara, in the western part of Mexico. Guadalajara is home to mariachi music, tequila, and the Mexican cowboys known as charros. It also has a lot to offer in terms of history, culture, natural beauty, and lively traditions. This travel guide will provide a comprehensive overview of the must-see attractions in Guadalajara and the Western region, including tequila tours, Tlaquepaque's art and traditions, the city's historic center, and Jalisco's natural wonders.

5.1 Exploring the Old Town of Guadalajara:
The Historic Center of Guadalajara is a treasure trove of amazing architecture that reflects the city's long history and colonial past. The main square, Plaza de Armas, is where you should start your exploration. Here, you can take in the stunning Guadalajara Cathedral. With its towering spires and intricate facade, the Spanish

Gothic cathedral is an impressive sight. The Jalisco Government Palace, also known as the Palacio de Gobierno, can be found nearby. It is adorned with breathtaking murals created by the well-known artist Jose Clemente Orozco.

Take a stroll down the pedestrian street known as Avenida Juarez, which is lined with beautiful buildings, cafes, and shops. Take a trip to the Essential World Heritage-listed Instituto Cultural Cabanas, which features incredible artwork and a roof terrace with breathtaking views. Take a look at the famous Orozco frescoes and contemporary art exhibits at the Hospicio Cabanas, an 18th-century orphanage that has been converted into a museum. One of Mexico's biggest markets is the Mercado Libertad, where you can buy traditional crafts and eat local street food.

5.2 Tastings and Tours of Tequila:

A tequila tour is a must on any trip to Guadalajara. To learn more about how Mexico's most popular drink is made, visit the town of Tequila, which is just a short drive from the city. Witness the traditional methods used to make tequila when you go to the renowned distilleries in the area, or "tequilas." Participate in guided tours that provide information on the agave plant cultivation, harvesting, and distillation processes. Learn to distinguish the flavors and qualities of various tequilas through tastings of Blanco, reposado, and also varieties. Make sure to pick up a few bottles to experience the authentic flavor of Mexico's national spirit.

5.3 Tlaquepaque's Art and Traditions:
Tlaquepaque is a charming town famous for its art and traditional Mexican crafts, and it is only a few kilometers from Guadalajara. Visit the galleries, boutiques, and craft workshops that line the pedestrian-friendly streets. Here, you can watch artisans at

work and buy one-of-a-kind handmade goods. Jardin Hidalgo, the main square, is a beautiful spot to unwind and listen to live music while sipping on local beverages. The impressive collection of traditional Mexican ceramics at the Museo Regional de la Ceramica highlights the region's rich pottery heritage.

By attending traditional folkloric dances and performances, you can fully immerse yourself in the vibrant traditions of Tlaquepaque. You shouldn't miss El Parian, the neighborhood market for craftspeople, where you can look at and buy beautiful handmade goods like pottery, blown glass, and clothing. For those who enjoy art and culture, Tlaquepaque is a must-visit destination due to its atmosphere, historic buildings, and artistic flair.

5.4 Seeing Jalisco's Natural Treasures:
The state of Jalisco is blessed with a variety of natural landscapes, making it possible for

tourists to view breathtaking mountains, vibrant forests, and unspoiled coastlines. You can see the wonders of the region within a few hours of driving from Guadalajara.

Go to the nature preserve known as Bosque La Primavera, which is just outside of Guadalajara. This natural haven features numerous hiking trails, soothing hot springs, and mesmerizing waterfalls, making it ideal for both adventure and relaxation. Take a dip in the revitalizing thermal waters, look for exotic birds and animals in the dense pine forests, and explore.

The Lake Chapala region, south of Guadalajara, is a popular destination for outdoor enthusiasts. The most expansive freshwater lake in Mexico, Lake Chapala, offers breathtaking views, boat rides, water sports, fishing trips, and more. Take a look at the charming lakeside towns of Ajijic and

Chapala, which are known for their vibrant local markets, vibrant architecture, and tranquil atmosphere. Take in the natural splendor of Jalisco's landscapes by hiking, riding a horse, and visiting the nearby mountains of Tapalpa and Mazamitla.

Conclusion:
Travelers can choose from a wide range of experiences and attractions in Guadalajara and the Western region of Mexico. This region has something for everyone, from seeing the amazing architecture and cultural landmarks of Guadalajara's historic center to taking tequila tours and tastings and immersing oneself in Tlaquepaque's art and traditions. In addition, the wonders of Jalisco's natural environment, such as the forests, mountains, and picturesque Lake Chapala, offer opportunities for outdoor recreation and adventure. By following this travel guide, visitors to Guadalajara and the Western region of Mexico can get the most out of their time there and leave with fond

memories of this culturally rich and naturally diverse destination.

YUCATÁN PENINSULA

7.1 The Colonial Past of Merida:

Merida, the state capital of Yucatan, is a vibrant city with a lot of colonial history. Merida, also known as the "White City," is a bustling city with stunning architecture and cobblestone streets. The city's numerous cathedrals, plazas, and mansions, which exhibit a combination of Spanish and Mayan influences, reflect its colonial charm.

The Plaza Grande, Merida's main square, is one of the city's must-see attractions. The magnificent Casa Montejo, an impressive mansion built in the 16th century, and the magnificent Cathedral of San Ildefonso, the oldest cathedral in the Americas, can both be seen here. You can get a glimpse into the day-to-day life of the locals by walking around the city and coming across vibrant houses, charming parks, and local markets.

Take advantage of the chance to explore the expansive Paseo de Montejo, a street lined with stunning French-style mansions and sculptures. You can appreciate Merida's architectural splendor by taking a stroll or bike ride along the avenue. Moreover, the neighborhood of St Nick Ana offers energetic and creative energy, with its numerous craftsmanship exhibitions, shops, and popular bistros.

Visit some of Merida's museums to fully experience the colonial past. The vast collection of Mayan artifacts on display at the Museum of Anthropology and History sheds light on the region's pre-Hispanic past. Contrasting the city's colonial architecture, the Yucatan Museum of Contemporary Art features contemporary works by local and international artists.

7.2 Antiquated Mayan Destinations: Uxmal, Chichen Itza:
Chichen Itza and Uxmal, both on the Yucatan Peninsula, are two of the most

well-known Mayan ruins, and no trip to Mexico is complete without seeing them.

Chichen Itza, assigned as a Essential World Legacy Site and one of the New Seven Miracles of the World, takes the stand concerning the significance of the Mayan progress. The Temple of Kukulcan, also known as El Castillo, is an iconic structure on the site. It is a pyramid with 91 steps on each side that represent the 365 days of the Mayan calendar. The Great Ball Court, where ancient Mayan sports competitions were held, and the Temple of Warriors, which is decorated with intricate carvings, can also be explored.

Although smaller than Chichen Itza, Uxmal, another Essential World Heritage Site, is equally impressive. Uxmal stands out because of its exceptionally well-preserved architecture, which features decorative motifs and intricate geometric designs. The Pyramid of the Entertainer, overwhelming the focal square, is an unquestionable necessity. Take as much time as necessary to investigate the Religious Shelter Quadrangle, the Lead representative's Royal residence, and the Place of the Turtles, all showing wonderful craftsmanship and a brief look into the old Mayan lifestyle.

7.3 Cenotes: Underground Normal Pools:

The Yucatan Landmass is popular for its cenotes, regular sinkholes shaped by the breakdown of limestone bedrock, uncovering perfect underground pools. Because they were regarded as sacred and were frequently used for rituals and ceremonies, these cenotes have a significant place in Mayan culture.

The unique experience of exploring cenotes includes swimming in crystal-clear waters and marveling at the stunning rock formations. The cenotes come in a variety of sizes and shapes, offering visitors a variety of experiences. While some cenotes are open-air and illuminated by sunlight, others are partially or completely underground, creating an ethereal atmosphere. The water in cenotes is frequently cool and refreshing, providing relief from the heat of the region.

Numerous tourists visit cenotes like Ik Kil, Dos Ojos, and Hubiku because they provide facilities like platforms, stairs, and even zip lines for those who are more daring. In some cenotes, snorkeling, and scuba diving are also popular activities that let visitors explore the underwater caves and see unusual rock formations like stalagmites and stalactites.

7.4 Valladolid and Izamal: Pueblo Mágicos:
The Mexican government has designated Izamal and Valladolid, two charming towns on the Yucatan Peninsula, as "Pueblo Mágicos," or "Magical Towns." These towns provide a glimpse into the colonial past, vibrant culture, and local customs of the region.

Because of its distinctive yellow-painted buildings, Izamal is referred to as the "Yellow City." The Convento de San Antonio de Padua, a massive Franciscan monastery built on top of an ancient Mayan pyramid, is the town's most important landmark. Climb to the top of the convent for sweeping views of the town and the beautiful courtyards that surround it. Izamal also has charming streets, plazas, and shops selling local crafts, making it a great place to wander around and soak up the atmosphere.

Another Pueblo Mágico, Valladolid, is known as the "Gateway to Chichen Itza." It has its special charm. The brilliant structures, tree-lined roads, and beautiful focal square add to the town's captivating environment. Explore the nearby Cenote Zaci, where you can unwind, swim, and take in the natural splendor, as well as the stunning Valladolid Cathedral, which was built in the 16th century. In addition, the town is well-known for its mouthwatering Yucatecan cuisine, with numerous local eateries serving up traditional dishes like salutes and cochinita pibil.

When compared to larger cities like Merida or Cancun, Izamal and Valladolid offer an experience that is more authentic and relaxed. They give you a glimpse of Mexico's colonial past, and you can truly experience the country's rich cultural heritage by wandering their streets and interacting with the friendly locals.

THE PACIFIC COAST AND BAJA CALIFORNIA

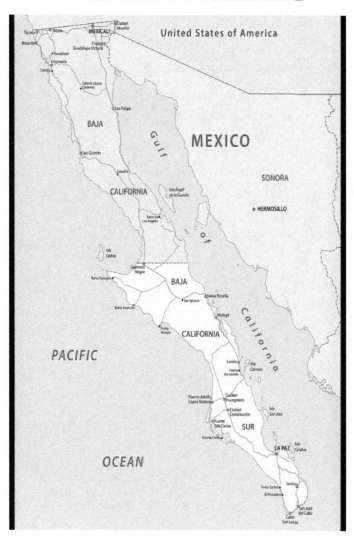

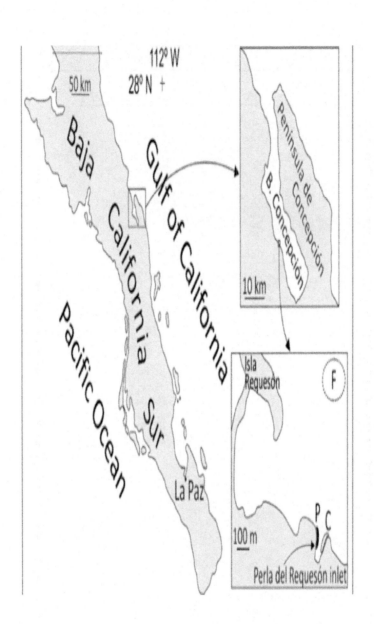

50 km

112° W
28° N +

Baja California Sur

Gulf of California

Pacific Ocean

La Paz

Península de Concepción

B. Concepción

10 km

Isla Requesón

F

P C

100 m

Perla del Requesón inlet

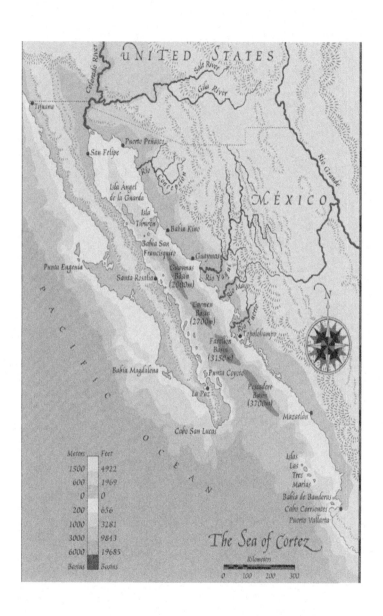

The Sea of Cortez

Meters	Feet
1500	4922
600	1969
0	0
200	656
1000	3281
3000	9843
6000	19685
Basins	Basins

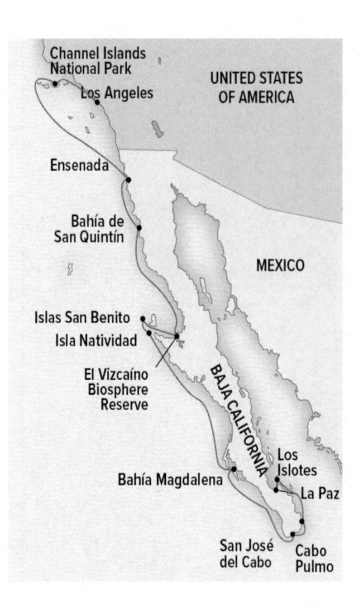

Channel Islands
National Park
Los Angeles

UNITED STATES
OF AMERICA

Ensenada

Bahía de
San Quintín

MEXICO

Islas San Benito
Isla Natividad

El Vizcaíno
Biosphere
Reserve

BAJA CALIFORNIA

Los
Islotes

Bahía Magdalena

La Paz

San José
del Cabo

Cabo
Pulmo

8.1 Puerto Vallarta and Riviera Nayarit:

Situated on the Pacific Shoreline of Mexico, Puerto Vallarta and Riviera Nayarit are famous vacation locations known for their dazzling sea shores, lively culture, and beautiful scenes. This region has something for everyone who wants to travel, thanks to its combination of natural beauty, rich history, and modern conveniences.

Puerto Vallarta, more commonly referred to as PV, is a charming coastal town that effortlessly combines traditional Mexican charm with contemporary developments. Cobblestone streets, vibrant buildings, and bustling markets make up El Centro, the downtown area. The famous Malecon, a beachfront promenade lined with shops, restaurants, and sculptures, can be explored by visitors here. Another must-see attraction in Puerto Vallarta is the eponymous Cathedral of Our Lady of Guadalupe, which features stunning architecture and a vibrant religious heritage.

Riviera Nayarit is a famous stretch of coastline north of Puerto Vallarta known for its opulent resorts, pristine beaches, and world-class golf courses. This region offers a more easygoing air, ideal for those looking for unwinding and serenity. In Riviera Nayarit, Bucerias and Sayulita are popular beach towns with beautiful stretches of sand, great surfing spots, and a bohemian vibe. Visitors to Bucerias can enjoy watersports like kayaking and snorkeling, fresh seafood at beachside restaurants, and a stroll through the town's art galleries.

The Marietas Islands National Park is a must-see for nature enthusiasts. This protected area of the Riviera Nayarit offers snorkeling, bird watching, and hidden beach exploration, including the well-known Playa Escondida, or Hidden Beach. The park's one-of-a-kind ecosystem and a wide range of marine life, including dolphins, sea turtles, and vibrant fish, are well-known.

8.2 Surfing in Punta de Mita and Sayulita:
Mexico's Riviera Nayarit towns of Sayulita and Punta de Mita are well-known surfing hotspots. Because of its consistent waves and vibrant surf culture, Sayulita in particular has gained popularity among surfers from all over the world. Sayulita has a variety of breaks for all levels, making it a great place for beginners to learn and for experienced surfers to test themselves. Visitors can easily get started and experience the thrill of surfing thanks to the abundance of surf schools and rental shops.

Punta de Mita, which is only a short drive from Sayulita, provides a more exclusive and secluded surfing environment. It is popular with professional surfers from all over the world due to its world-class breaks like El Anclote and La Lancha. Additionally, the region is home to several high-end beach clubs and resorts, making it an ideal location for surfers seeking a location with both exceptional waves and high-end amenities.

Both Sayulita and Punta de Mita offer laid-back ocean-side energy, with various beachside cafés and shops taking special care of surfers and sightseers. Following a day of riding the waves, guests can appreciate scrumptious fish dishes, reviving drinks, and take in the staggering dusks, making Sayulita and Punta de Mita ideal objections for ocean side and surf lovers.

8.3 Observing Whales in Baja California:
The spectacular opportunities for whale watching in Baja California, in the northwest of Mexico, have earned it a reputation for themselves. One of the best places in the world to witness the impressive migration of gray whales is on Baja California's Pacific coast, where thousands of them spend the winter.

The town of Guerrero Negro, arranged in the core of Baja California, is a well-known beginning stage for whale-watching journeys. Visitors can take boat tours led by knowledgeable guides to learn more about these magnificent creatures' biology and behavior. As the boat travels through the quiet waters of the Ojo de Liebre tidal pond, otherwise called Scammon's Tidal Pond, guests can observe dark whales penetrating, rambling water, and, surprisingly, coming up near the boat. Observing these gentle giants in their natural environment is awe-inspiring.

The town of San Ignacio, which is further south in Baja California, is another popular place to watch whales. This locale is known for experiences with agreeable and inquisitive dim whale moms and their calves. Guests can join directed visits that permit them to get very close to these glorious animals, frequently bringing about extraordinary and inspiring associations.

Gray whales migrate to the warm waters of Baja California from their feeding grounds in the Arctic to mate and give birth during the whale-watching season, which typically runs from December to April. Numerous tour operators offer whale-watching excursions during this time, guaranteeing visitors an unforgettable and one-of-a-kind experience.

8.4 Exploring La Paz and Todos Santos:
On the Baja California Peninsula, the cities of Todos Santos and La Paz show a different side of Mexico with their stunning desert landscapes, extensive cultural heritage, and laid-back atmosphere.

To all of Santos, also known as the "Magic Town" or "Pueblo Magico," is a charming haven between the Pacific Ocean and the Sierra de la Laguna mountains. The town is known for its imaginative local area, notable structures, and pleasant roads fixed with exhibitions, stores, and bistros. The local art galleries, the historic mission church, and delectable regional cuisine await visitors. Todos Santos's pristine beaches are within easy reach, making them ideal for swimming, surfing, or just basking in the rays.

The capital of Baja California Sur, La Paz, combines old-world charm with modern conveniences. A must-see attraction in La Paz is The Malecon, a waterfront promenade with stunning views of the Sea of Cortez, vibrant street art, and a variety of seafood-serving restaurants. Colonial architecture, lively markets, and a buzzing atmosphere characterize the historic downtown area. Espiritu Santo Island, a Essential World Heritage Site known for its crystal-clear waters, an abundance of marine life, and excellent snorkeling opportunities, can also be reached by boat tour.

Both Tasks Santos and La Paz are known for their normal magnificence, with various open doors for outside exercises. Guests can investigate the encompassing desert scenes, go climbing or trekking, and even spot one-of-a-kind untamed life, like dolphins, ocean lions, and whale sharks, in the close by waters. Todos Santos and La Paz have a wide range of activities for tourists to choose from, including cultural immersion, outdoor adventures, and relaxation.

FOOD AND DRINK IN MEXICO

145

9.1 Conventional Mexican Cooking:

Conventional Mexican cooking is rich and varied, addressing the combination of various native and European culinary practices. One of the most significant dishes is unquestionably the scrumptious tacos. These scrumptious handheld treats comprise a delicate corn tortilla loaded up with different fixings. From delicious barbecued steak to delicate sluggish cooked pork, tacos come in endless varieties and are much of the time joined by lively salsas, new cilantro, and tart lime.

One more staple of Mexican cooking is the generous and ameliorating mole. Mole is a mind-boggling sauce made with a mix of bean stew peppers, chocolate, nuts, seeds, and a horde of flavors. The outcome is an orchestra of flavors, going from smoky to sweet and zesty. Frequently presented with delicate chicken or turkey, mole is a genuine delicacy that can be tracked down in numerous territorial varieties the nation over.

For those looking for an explosion of newness, ceviche is a well-known decision. Made with new crude seafood marinated in lime juice, ceviche is ordinarily blended in with diced tomatoes, onions, cilantro, and avocado. This zingy dish is an ideal counteractant to the warm Mexican climate and is generally delighted in as a hors d'oeuvre or light lunch.

To fulfill your sweet tooth, enjoy a few conventional pastries like churros and flan. Churros are a fresh broiled mixture of baked goods covered in cinnamon sugar that are frequently delighted in with a warm cup of chocolate for plunging. Then again, flan is a delectable caramel custard dessert that is smooth and an exemplary method for finishing dinner in Mexico.

9.2 Road Food and Markets:

An excursion to Mexico wouldn't be finished without encountering the enticing universe of Mexican road food. Strolling through the clamoring roads, you will experience energetic food slows down and trucks offering a wide cluster of scrumptious dishes. One well-known road food thing is elite, which comprises barbecued old-fashioned corn slathered with mayo, sprinkled with cheddar, and bean stew powder, and presented with a crush of lime. Its blend of velvety, smoky, and zesty flavors is essentially overpowering.

Wandering further, you'll run over antojitos, which means "little desires." These little nibbles incorporate top choices like tamales, gorditas, and quesadillas. Tamales are produced using masa (corn-based mixture) loaded up with different exquisite or sweet fillings, enveloped by a corn husk, and steamed. Gorditas are thick tortillas loaded down with appetizing fillings like beans, cheddar, or meat, while quesadillas are tortillas loaded up with cheddar and different fixings and barbecued to gooey flawlessness.

Investigating neighborhood markets, like Mercado de San Juan in Mexico City or Mercado Metropolitan in Oaxaca, is an outright unquestionable requirement for food aficionados. These clamoring markets offer an overflow of new products, flavors, meats, and neighborhood indulgences. You can test extraordinary natural products like guanabana or attempt the wide assortment of territorial cheeses and salsas. The market's enthusiastic environment, clamoring with local people, and the captivating fragrances of newly prepared food, genuinely submerge you in the legitimate culinary culture of Mexico.

9.3 Territorial Claims to Fame and Eateries: Mexico's territorial cooking styles are pretty much as different as its scenes, permitting you to set out on a gastronomic excursion all through the country. From the beachfront districts to the high countries and in the middle between, every territory values its one-of-a-kind claims to fame.

In the Yucatan Promontory, appreciate the unmistakable kinds of Mayan cooking. Cochinita pibil, a conventional dish from this district, comprises of marinated pork slow-cooked in a banana leaf, bringing about delicate and delightful meat. Match it with certain tart salted onions and habanero salsa for a genuinely legitimate Yucatecan experience.

In the territory of Oaxaca, enjoy the rich and complex kinds of its cooking. Test the notorious mole negro, a profound and dull mole made with a few kinds of bean stew peppers, chocolate, nuts, and sweet-smelling flavors. The outcome is a smooth sauce that delightfully covers delicate bits of chicken or tortillas, offering a blast of flavors that will leave you needing more.

Moving to the beachfront districts, don't pass up the impeccable seafood contributions. In Baja California, savor the experience of fish and shrimp tacos loaded up with new off-the-boat get that has been flawlessly prepared and barbecued. Presented with a crush of lime and joined by an invigorating pico de gallo salsa, these tacos are a genuine enjoyment for seafood sweethearts.

Mexico is additionally home to various top-notch eateries that proposition refined understandings of conventional dishes. Pujol, situated in Mexico City, is viewed as quite possibly of the best eatery on the planet. Its imaginative interpretation of conventional Mexican fixings and procedures makes a feasting experience that is both refined and well-established in Mexican culinary practices. Another significant foundation is Quintonil, which grandstands the variety of Mexican fixings in both conventional and cutting-edge dishes.

9.4 Tequila, Mezcal, and Mexican Refreshments:

Mexico is prestigious for its development of tequila and mezcal, two notorious refined spirits with rich social importance. Tequila is produced using the blue agave plant, fundamentally delivered in the territory of Jalisco. It very well may be delighted in different structures, including as a straight shot joined by a cut of lime and a touch of salt, or in mixed drinks like the reviving Margarita or the exemplary Tequila Dawn.

Mezcal, then again, is refined from the core of the agave plant, known as the piña. What separates mezcal is its smoky flavor, accomplished through the conventional technique for slow-simmering the agave hearts in underground pits. Tasting on mezcal permits you to appreciate the high-quality craftsmanship and the unmistakable person of this extraordinary soul.

Besides these spirits, Mexico offers a variety of other conventional refreshments. One well-known decision is horchata, an invigorating beverage produced using a blend of ground rice or almonds, water, sugar, and cinnamon. Its velvety surface and unpretentious pleasantness give an ideal reprieve from the intensity.

On the off chance that you're needing a caffeine fix, attempt the conventional Mexican espresso known as Bistro de Olla. This sweet-smelling espresso is fermented with cinnamon and piloncillo (crude sweetener), giving it a particularly rich and delightful taste.

Generally speaking, Mexico's culinary scene is an excursion that embraces both practice and development. From energetic road food to the best feasting foundations, the nation offers a gastronomic encounter that will leave your taste buds asking for more. In this way, let your faculties be directed by the tempting fragrances, energetic varieties, and different flavors that characterize Mexican food and beverages, and get ready for a culinary experience like no other.

OUTDOOR ADVENTURE AND NATURE IN MEXICO

10.1 Sierra Madre Climbing and Hiking:

A treasured paradise for adventurers can be found in Mexico's center; the magnificent Sierra Madre range of mountains. A world of unparalleled beauty and thrilling exploration awaits as you ascend into the tranquil embrace of these rugged peaks. Prepare to lose yourself in the enchanting wilderness by lacing up your hiking boots and packing your supplies.

There are a lot of hiking trails in the Sierra Madre, each with its own experience. The intoxicating scent of pine trees fills the air as you begin your ascent, and your eyes feast on panoramic views of rolling hills that stretch as far as the eye can see. The paths wind through thick backwoods, disclosing beautiful glades sprouting with lively wildflowers, and crossing completely clear streams that murmur insider facts of the land.

The Sierra Madre has a lot of difficult climbing routes for people who want to go on more daring adventures. You conquer each ledge, rewarded with breathtaking views that make every sweat worth it, as your hands grip the weathered rocks and your heart races. The Sierra Madre inspires exploration with its towering mountains and jagged cliffs, leaving you breathless not only from the climb but also from the sheer magnitude of its natural wonders.

10.2 Scenic Caves and Waterfalls:

Mexico's scenic waterfalls and enigmatic caves beckon you into their secret world beyond the dense forests and hidden trails of the Sierra Madre. Prepare to be captivated by their raw power and ethereal beauty.

Every step you take as you get closer to a cascading waterfall builds anticipation. A mesmerizing spray that kisses your skin is created when the vibrant emerald water hits the rocks. You are enveloped by the ethereal mist, and you feel free and connected to nature. The experience leaves an indelible mark on your soul whether you choose to swim in the cool pools below the falls or simply stand in awe.

A maze of caves that have long captivated readers with tales of awe and mystery can be found deeper into Mexico's natural wonders. The temperature drops with each step, and the world around you changes into one that is dark. Stalactites and stalagmites create otherworldly sculptures that pique the imagination and hang from the ceiling and floor. As you investigate these old caves and their secret chambers, you feel a feeling of worship for the World's secret profundities, a sign of the gigantic miracles that lie underneath our feet.

10.3 Wildlife Reserves and Sanctuary:

When you enter the meticulously preserved sanctuaries and reserves of Mexico, you will be immersed in the vibrant tapestry of the country's wildlife. In these secure havens, where humans and animals live in harmony with one another, you can see nature at its most exquisite.

As you enter the sanctuary, the sound of birdsong draws you into their world, where a rainbow of colors awaits. Exotic species dance delicately among the trees, their melodious calls harmonizing to form a natural symphony of beauty. You might come across a rare Mexican grey wolf or a majestic jaguar as you wander through these diverse ecosystems, which will serve as a reminder of how crucial it is to preserve these animals for future generations.

10.4 Exciting Activities: Rafting, zip lining, and more:

Mexico has heart-pounding adventure sports for thrill seekers and adrenaline junkies that will make your heart race and leave you breathless for more. As you zip line above the forest floor through lush canopies, prepare for an exhilarating ride through the trees.

Be that as it may, the adrenaline doesn't stop there. Navigate the raging rapids of Mexico's wild rivers with a paddle. As you maneuver through twirling eddies and towering waves, the raging waters test your skills. Few other activities can compare to the exhilaration of conquering a turbulent river.

If that isn't enough, don your gear and go diving into the ocean's depths to see vibrant coral reefs where marine life dances in a rainbow of colors. Scuba diving or snorkeling in the warm waters of Mexico will take you to an underwater paradise where you will have an unforgettable encounter with exotic sea creatures.

The adventure sports available in Mexico are an invitation to test your limits, revel in the excitement, and savor the nectar of life. You'll come away from each activity with stories of exhilaration to tell for the rest of your life.

FESTIVALS AND CELEBRATIONS IN MEXICO

11.1 The Deadly Day:

The Day of the Dead, also known as Dia de los Muertos in local Spanish, is one of Mexico's most famous and distinctive celebrations. This extraordinary festival, which takes place every year from October 31 to November 2, is a vibrant and colorful tribute to loved ones who have passed away.

Mexicans believe that the spirits of the deceased visit Earth during this time to reunite with their loved ones. The celebrations combine Catholic traditions with ancient Aztec practices to create a rich tapestry of rituals, food, decorations, and parades.

In different locales of Mexico, families accumulate in burial grounds to clean and beautify the graves of their family members. They construct intricate altars, or ofrendas, adorned with marigolds, candles, photographs, favored foods, and the deceased's cherished possessions. It is believed that these offerings encourage the spirits to return to the living world.

Processions and parades bring the city's streets to life with music, elaborate costumes, and elaborate skull-face makeup. Sugar skulls, masks, colorful decorations, and intricate sculptures all feature skulls and skeletons, which are iconic Day of the Dead symbols.

Families prepare traditional dishes that hold a lot of significance as part of this lively celebration. During this time, Pan de Muerto, a sweet bread shaped like bones and coated in sugar, is a staple. Families meet up to cook tamales, moles, and other provincial indulgences to share and respect their withdrawn friends and family.

During the Day of the Dead, if you happen to be in Mexico City, Oaxaca, or any other town in the country, you will undoubtedly have an unforgettable, moving experience. This celebration is one to never forget because of the vibrant colors, a strong sense of community, joyful music, and sincere reflection.

11.2   Celebrations   commemorating Independence Day:

One of Mexico's most significant holidays is Independence Day, which falls on September 16th. This significant occasion marks the country's declaration of independence from Spanish colonial rule by Miguel Hidalgo in 1810. The celebrations last longer than just one day, frequently lasting up to a week.

The streets of Mexico are alive with excitement leading up to Independence Day. The Mexican flag's three primary colors — red, white, and green — are displayed on public buildings, homes, and other structures. It is impossible to miss the patriotic atmosphere that permeates the nation, from bustling markets to town squares.

The night known as El Grito de Independencia (The Cry of Independence) occurs on September 15th. Political figures and local leaders reenact Hidalgo's well-known "call to arms" in front of large crowds in town squares. "Viva Mexico!" is chanted along by the crowd. The national anthem is sung with great enthusiasm at eleven, and fireworks light up the sky to signify the beginning of the celebration.

The next day, September sixteenth, is an authority occasion, and urban areas across Mexico have marches, shows, and customary moves. Groups play mariachi music, which is symbolic of Mexican culture, while individuals in intricate ensembles walk through the roads. There is a shared sense of enthusiasm and pride for the country's independence in the air.

Freedom Day is much of the time an event to enjoy customary Mexican dishes, for example, chiles en nogada, a bubbly dish comprising of poblano peppers loaded down with ground meat and embellished with a velvety pecan sauce and pomegranate seeds. Tacos, tamales, and grilled corn on the cob are just a few of the delicious dishes offered by street vendors.

During the Independence Day celebrations, the Mexican people's passion and devotion to their country are palpable. It is a joyful and patriotic occasion that exemplifies the resilience, culture, and history of the nation.

11.3 Oaxacan Guelaguetza:

The magnificent Guelaguetza celebration is located in the center of Oaxaca, one of Mexico's most culturally diverse states. This indigenous extravaganza, which takes place each year in July, showcases the diverse ethnic groups that call Oaxaca home with their elaborate customs, vibrant costumes, and traditional dances.

Guelaguetza, which can be translated as "offering" or "gift," is a gathering of indigenous people to show the world their traditional music, dance, and rituals. The festival, which dates back to the pre-Hispanic period and is deeply entwined with Oaxaca's indigenous heritage, is an exceptional cultural experience for both locals and tourists.

The Cerro del Fortin, the city's auditorium, hosts the festival on two Mondays in a row. Artists from different networks, wearing intricate, beautiful outfits addressing their one-of-a-kind customs, become the dominant focal point. The moves are joined by the throbbing rhythms of conventional instruments, including Zapotec drums, woodwinds, and marimbas.

The wide variety of traditional costumes on display is one of Guelaguetza's most captivating features. Huipiles, skirts, and headdresses embellished with flowers and feathers are worn by women. Men flaunt their impressive charro attire, which includes leather chaps, embroidered jackets, and wide-brimmed hats.

Guelaguetza is a chance to taste the flavors of Oaxaca in addition to the dance performances. Tlayudas (giant, crispy tortillas topped with a variety of ingredients), mole (Oaxaca's famous, complex sauce), and mezcal (the iconic local spirit) are among the tempting regional delicacies available at food stalls.

In addition to being a celebration of Oaxaca's indigenous culture, the Guelaguetza festival is a reminder of the resilience and pride of its people. The richness of Oaxacan traditions is imprinted on the souls of all visitors who are fortunate enough to participate in this immersive experience.

11.4 Religious and Carnival Processions:

Mexico is famous for its lively merriments, and the festival is among the most enthusiastically expected occasions. Celebrated in the weeks paving the way to Loaned, the fair is a period of parties, marches, and concealed festivals that mirror the country's solid Catholic legacy.

Various urban communities all through Mexico have their remarkable approach to praising fair, however, Veracruz and Mazatlan stand apart as two of the most renowned amusement park objections in the country.

In Veracruz, this spectacle goes on for nine days and is a combination of pre-Hispanic, Spanish, and Afro-Caribbean customs. The streets of the city are covered in bright decorations, and the air is filled with the infectious beat of Latin music. A festive atmosphere that encompasses the entire city is created by parades that feature spectacular floats, dancers, and acrobats.

On the other hand, Mazatlan is home to one of Mexico's largest carnivals. This waterfront town wakes up for seven days in lengthy festivity loaded up with music, moving, and elaborate ensembles. The crowning of the carnival queen, who takes on the role of festival leader, is the highlight. The streets are filled with spectacular parades that leave behind a trail of joy and celebration.

Mexican culture also includes religious processions, which are especially popular during Holy Week, the week before Easter. In celebration of Jesus Christ's crucifixion and resurrection, processions transform the streets of the nation into sacred paths.

Intricately patterned carpets made of sawdust, flower petals, and other natural materials adorn the streets in vibrant colors. While singing hymns and praying, participants in religious robes carry saint statues, crucifixes, and religious artifacts.

These religious events, from the processions in Taxco lit by candles to the Passion Play in Iztapalapa, show the devotion and faith of the Mexican people.

In general, a myriad of captivating celebrations and customs make up Mexico's rich cultural tapestry. Mexico offers a one-of-a-kind travel experience filled with vibrant colors, captivating dances, melodious music, and profound cultural significance, whether it's the enchanting Day of the Dead, the patriotic Independence Day celebrations, the awe-inspiring Guelaguetza, or the joyous carnivals and religious processions.

SHOPPING AND SOUVENIRS IN MEXICO

12.1 Artisans and Traditional Crafts:

Traditional artisans and craftsmen are crucial to the preservation of Mexico's extensive cultural heritage. These local artisans produce works of art that are stunningly intricate and vibrant by utilizing ancient methods that have been handed down through the generations.

The art of "alebrijes" is one of Mexico's most famous traditional crafts. The whimsical, brightly colored wooden carvings have fanciful creatures and intricate details. Alebrijes are especially well-known among artisans in the state of Oaxaca's small town of San Martn Tilcajete. Guests can observe the interaction firsthand by visiting the nearby studios, where craftsmen enthusiastically cut, paint, and embellish every special piece.

One more customary specialty that Mexico is known for is silver adornments. In the charming town of Taxco, which is in the Guerrero state, there are a lot of shops and workshops that are all about making silver. This precious metal is made into beautiful necklaces, earrings, bracelets, and other pieces of art that can be worn by skilled craftsmen. The exceptional quality and timeless designs of Taxco's silver jewelry make it a must-visit destination for jewelry enthusiasts.

12.2 Carefully assembled Materials and Earthenware:

Handmade textiles from a wide range of regions are found in Mexico, reflecting the country's diverse cultural traditions. The province of Chiapas is popular for its vivid materials, overwhelmingly made by native networks. In San Cristóbal de las Casas, the principal market flourishes with dynamic materials, for example, complicatedly woven huipiles (conventional shirts) and rebozos (cloaks). Visitors can see how to weave on a traditional backstrap loom and buy one-of-a-kind handcrafted textiles directly from the artisans.

Additionally, Oaxaca is well-known for its exceptional pottery. Pottery is expertly made in Oaxaca by skilled artisans using centuries-old methods. The town of St Nick María Atzompa is eminent for its green-coated earthenware. Meander through the studios and notice the dominance of the potters as they shape and form wonderful jars, plates, and other earthenware pieces. By purchasing these handicrafts, tourists can take home a piece of Oaxacan culture and craftsmanship.

12.3 Markets and Shopping Streets:

For those who appreciate one-of-a-kind, handcrafted items, Mexico's shopping streets, and markets are a haven. Numerous high-end boutiques and designer stores can be found on Mexico City's bustling Avenida Presidente Masaryk. Mexican designer shops as well as international brands can be found here, selling chic clothing, accessories, and home decor.

There are numerous markets in San Miguel de Allende, a Essential World Heritage Site, that cater to a wide range of eclectic tastes. Leather goods, ceramics, textiles, and souvenirs are just a few of the colorful handmade crafts available at the Mercado de Artesanas. You can find hidden treasures that are a reflection of San Miguel de Allende's vibrant artistic community as you stroll through its streets and markets.

12.4 Special Mexican Memorabilia:

Mexico provides a plethora of options for unique souvenirs. One of the most notable Mexican keepsakes is the conventional Mexican sombrero. These wide-overflowed caps, frequently decorated with bright weaving and examples, make for an ideal remembrance to recall your Mexican experience.

For those looking for culinary pleasure, Mexican flavors, for example, stew powder and Mexican vanilla, make astounding keepsakes. After your trip, these real flavors will take you back to the vibrant flavors of Mexico.

Additionally, Puebla's hand-painted Talavera pottery is an exquisite option for a souvenir. This vibrant piece of ceramic art is a symbol of Mexico's colonial past and is characterized by its blue and white designs. It can be found in the local markets and shops of Puebla.

Lastly, mezcal, a prized Mexican liquor that is gaining international recognition as a distinct type of tequila made from agave, is gaining popularity. You'll be able to remember your time in Mexico forever if you bring home a bottle of mezcal to share with friends and family.

Mexico offers an immersive experience that celebrates its vibrant culture and skilled artisans, whether through its intricate crafts, textiles, bustling markets, or one-of-a-kind souvenirs. During your travels, take advantage of the chance to learn about this fascinating cultural aspect and treasure the unique memories and keepsakes you bring back.

LANGUAGE AND CULTURE TIPS IN MEXICO

13.1 Basic Spanish Phrases:

While traveling to Mexico, it is useful to gain proficiency with a few basic Spanish phrases to navigate through the country. Mexicans appreciate it when tourists try to communicate in their language. Here are a few essential phrases to memorize:

1. Hola - Hello
2. Buenos días - Good morning
3. Buenas tardes - Good afternoon
4. Buenas noches - Good evening
5. Por favor - Please
6. Gracias - Thank you
7. De nada - You're welcome
8. ¿Cómo estás? - How are you?
9. ¿Dónde está ...? - Where is ...?
10. Quisiera ... - I would like ...
11. No comprendo - I don't understand

12. ¿Cuánto cuesta? - How much does it cost?

13. ¿Dónde está el baño? - Where is the bathroom?

14. Perdón - Excuse me

15. Adiós - Goodbye

Practicing these phrases will greatly improve your travel experience in Mexico, as local people will recognize your effort and be more willing to assist you.

13.2 Mexican Etiquette and Customs:

Mexicans are known for their warm hospitality and polite habits. To blend in and show respect for the neighborhood culture, it is important to know about Mexican etiquette and customs.

1. Greetings: Mexicans greet by shaking hands or kissing on the cheek (for the most part between friends or family).

2. Punctuality: While being on time is appreciated, it is normal for social events to

start later than scheduled, so it is acceptable to arrive a couple of moments late.

3. Individual Space: Mexicans stand more like each other while conversing compared to a few other cultures. It is normal to maintain a shorter individual space bubble.

4. Eye-to-eye connection: Maintaining eye-to-eye connection during a conversation is a sign of respect and attentiveness.

5. Politeness: Use "por favor" (please) and "gracias" (thank you) frequently. Mexicans are for the most part polite and appreciate courtesy.

6. Dining Etiquette: It is customary to wait for the host to start eating, and it is polite to finish everything on your plate as it indicates you enjoyed the dinner.

7. Tipping: Tipping is expected in Mexico. A typical tip is around 10-15% of the total bill except if a service charge is already included.

8. Religion: Mexico is a predominantly Catholic country, so it is important to be

respectful while visiting places of worship or religious sites.

By being aware of and respecting these customs, you will contribute to building positive interactions and relationships during your visit to Mexico.

13.3 Understanding Mexican Traditions:
Mexico is a country rich in cultural traditions that are deeply rooted in history and hold great significance to its kin. Understanding these traditions will permit you to appreciate the cultural heritage of Mexico. Here are a couple of Mexican traditions worth exploring:

1. Day of the Dead (Día de los Muertos): This is a vibrant and heartfelt celebration held on November 1st and 2nd every year. Mexicans honor their deceased loved ones by building altars, decorating graves, and sharing their favorite food and drinks.

2. Mariachi Music: Originating in the state of Jalisco, Mariachi is a traditional Mexican music genre. The lively rhythms and emotional melodies of Mariachi bands are an integral part of Mexican celebrations and festivals.

3. Cinco de Mayo: Often mistaken as Mexico's Independence Day (which is celebrated on September 16), Cinco de Mayo commemorates the Mexican armed force's victory over France in the Battle of Puebla. It is celebrated with parades, traditional dances, and feasts.

4. Lucha Libre: Mexican wrestling is not just a sport but likewise a unique type of entertainment. With wrestlers wearing vibrant covers and performing acrobatic moves, Lucha Libre matches are an exhilarating experience that showcases Mexican passion and athleticism.

5. Las Posadas: This nine-day celebration leading up to Christmas reenacts the excursion of Mary and Joseph searching for a spot to stay. Every night, individuals

gather to go from one house to another, singing and reenacting the story, before enjoying traditional food and drinks.

These are just a couple of instances of Mexico's rich traditions. Exploring and participating in these customs will immerse you in the vibrant cultural fabric of Mexico.

13.4 Celebrating Mexican Holidays:
Mexicans are known for their vibrant and festive holiday celebrations. Embracing these occasions will permit you to experience the true quintessence of Mexican culture. Here are a few significant holidays that are widely celebrated in Mexico:

1. Independence Day (Día de la Independencia): On September 16th, Mexico celebrates its independence from Spain. Festivities include parades, concerts, fireworks, and the well-known Grito de Dolores (a reenactment of Miguel Hidalgo's weep for independence).

2. Christmas (Navidad): Christmas in Mexico is a magical time. The celebrations begin on December 12th with the feast of Our Lady of Guadalupe and culminate on Christmas Eve (Nochebuena). Families gather for a late-night dinner, midnight mass, and to trade gifts.

3. Semana Santa (Heavenly Week): This week leading up to Easter is observed with great devotion in Mexico. It involves processions, reenactments of the Passion of Christ, and vibrant street markets selling traditional food and crafts.

4. Day of the Kings (Día de Reyes): Celebrated on January 6th, this holiday denotes the end of the Christmas season. Children receive gifts and partake in the traditional Rosca de Reyes, a sweet bread with hidden figurines representing the child Jesus.

5. Revolution Day (Día de la Revolución): On November 20th, Mexico commemorates the start of the Mexican Revolution. Parades, historical reenactments, and

patriotic ceremonies take place the nation over.

By participating in these holiday celebrations, you will witness the delight, deep-rooted traditions, and festive spirit that are at the heart of Mexican culture.

In conclusion, armed with basic Spanish phrases, an understanding of Mexican etiquette and customs, knowledge of Mexican traditions, and the spirit to embrace their vibrant holiday celebrations, your excursion through Mexico will be enriched with authentic experiences and memories that will last a lifetime.

TRAVELING WITH CHILDREN TO MEXICO

Family-Friendly Destinations Mexico, with its diverse landscapes, cultural diversity, and warm hospitality, has a lot of family-friendly destinations that promise to make your vacation one to remember for everyone, young and old.

1. Cancun: For families, this well-known beach destination is a haven. Cancun is the ideal destination for sunbathers seeking an unforgettable beach experience because of its pristine shores, turquoise waters, and numerous all-inclusive resorts with exclusive family amenities.

2. Costa Maya: Only south of Cancun, the Riviera Maya is eminent for its dazzling sea shores and the popular Mayan remnants of Tulum. In the natural parks nearby, families

can have fun swimming with dolphins, exploring underwater cenotes, or embarking on an exciting eco-adventure.

3. City of Mexico: The energetic capital city isn't just a social center yet, in addition, it is a gold mine of attractions for families. Explore ancient sites like Teotihuacan, world-renowned museums like the National Museum of Anthropology, and Chapultepec Park, one of the world's largest urban parks, to immerse yourself in history.

4. Puerto Vallarta: Puerto Vallarta, which is located on the Pacific coast of Mexico, has a stunning combination of stunning beaches, lush jungles, and charming old town streets. Families can participate in a variety of watersports, including whale watching, snorkeling, and taking a boat tour to the Marietas Islands, which are known for their secret beaches.

2. Section 14: Attractions and Activities Suitable for Children Xcaret Park: Xcaret is an eco-park in Riviera Maya that combines nature, culture, and entertainment. Exploring the Mayan Village, where they can learn about ancient customs, floating in natural pools, and swimming in underground rivers are all activities that kids will adore.

2. Xel-Ha Park: One more diamond in Riviera Maya, Xel-Ha is a characteristic aquarium known for its swimming and swimming encounters. Children can swim around colorful fish in safety or go on a jungle hike to learn about the plants and animals in the area.

3. Boardwalk at El Malecon: The charming seaside promenade of Puerto Vallarta's Malecon features lively street performances, outdoor sculptures, and market stalls. The breathtaking views of the ocean and the

numerous art installations spread out along its length will entice children.

4. Papalote Children's Museum: The Papalote Children's Museum in Mexico City is a place where kids can learn about science, art, technology, and culture through interactive activities. There are hands-on exhibits, a 3D theater, and a planetarium at the museum.

In Section 14.3, Essentials for Traveling and Safety Tips Read the travel advisory from your home country's foreign office before going to Mexico and take any necessary precautions.

2. Avoid displaying flashy items or expensive jewelry. Utilize hotel safes whenever possible to safeguard your valuables.

3. Keep hydrated and use sunscreen, especially when you're at the beach because the sun in Mexico can be very strong.

4. Avoid calling random taxis on the street and instead use dependable modes of transportation. Settle trustworthy taxi organizations or ride-sharing applications.

Area 14.4: How to Plan a Memorable Family Vacation 1. Include your kids in the excursion arranging process by exploring attractions and exercises together. This piques their interest and enables them to take responsibility for their experiences.

2. Ensure that everyone has something to look forward to during the trip by planning a variety of activities that are appropriate for different age groups.

3. Your itinerary should be flexible enough to accommodate unexpected discoveries or spontaneous adventures.

4. Include comfortable clothing, swimwear, insect repellent, and any necessary medications in your packing list. Furthermore, convey a little emergency treatment unit and consistently have a duplicate of significant records like identifications and travel protection.

Your family will discover the wonders of this diverse nation and make memories that will last a lifetime if you follow the recommendations in this comprehensive Mexico travel guidebook. Mexico has everything you need for an unforgettable family vacation: warm Mexican hospitality, exploring ancient ruins, unwinding on breathtaking beaches, and immersing yourself in the vibrant culture.

APPENDIX

15.1 Vocabulary in Mexican:

Ⅰt can be helpful to familiarize yourself with some typical Mexican vocabulary before going to Mexico. To help you along your journey, here are a few key terms and phrases:

- Good tidings: " Hola" (Hi), "Buenos días" (Hello), "Buenas tardes" (Good evening), "Buenas noches" (Great night/night).

- Many thanks: " Gracias."

- Please: " Thank you."

Please excuse me: "Disculpe" or "Perdón."

- Yes: " Sí."

- No: " No."

- Farewell: " Adiós."

- "¿Dónde está...?" : " Where is...?"

- Bathroom: " Baño."

- The restaurant: Restaurante."

- Hotel: " Hotel."

- Beach: " Playa."

Don't be afraid to ask for help in English if you need it because many Mexicans are bilingual, especially in tourist-heavy regions. Be that as it may, displaying a work to convey in Spanish will constantly be valued by local people.

15.2 Important Phone Numbers and Contacts for Emergencies:

While investigating Mexico, realizing significant telephone numbers and crisis contacts can give true serenity. In the event of any unforeseen circumstances, keep these numbers handy:

- Fire, medical, and police emergency services: Dial 911.

- Traveler Help Hotline: 01-800-903-9200. Support and assistance geared specifically toward tourists are provided by this hotline.

- A consular or embassy: Find the Mexican embassy or consulate's phone number and address online. In the event of an emergency, they can offer you consular services or any other assistance you require.

15.3 Transportation Maps and Routes:

Getting around Mexico is made easier by the country's numerous transportation options. It is essential to have access to maps and transportation routes to effectively navigate. Some resources you might find useful are as follows:

- Maps Online: To locate comprehensive maps of Mexican towns and cities, make use of online resources like MapQuest, Apple Maps, and Google Maps. Directions, options for public transportation, and estimated travel times can all be provided by these apps in real-time.

- Textbooks: Maps and directions to major Mexican cities and popular tourist destinations can be found in a lot of travel guides. Take a look at the book's supplement for definite guides and suggested courses.

- Centers for Tourism Information: At the point when you show up in Mexico, visit nearby the travel industry data focuses, typically situated in air terminals or famous vacation regions. Free brochures, maps, and tailored guidance on transportation options for your needs are available from these centers.

15.4 Apps and Books to Try:

There are a lot of books, websites, and apps that can help you get the most out of your trip to Mexico. Here are some suggestions:

- Books:
  - "A Must-Read Mexico Travel Guide For First Time Visiting," published by Travel Guide Publishers, as well as other travel guides published by Travel Guide Publishers and other Authors.

- Apps:
  - Translator of Languages: By translating English phrases into Spanish and vice versa, you can easily communicate with the locals.
  - Cover for Currency: Keep up with the rates of currency exchange.

Apps for booking carbs: a safe and convenient means of getting around Mexican cities.

- HomeAway: Track down special facilities and encounters in Mexico.

You'll have access to a wealth of information to help you get the most out of your trip to Mexico if you use these resources.

<u>Thanks For Reading...</u>

Thanks for reading our Mexico travel guide book. You can get more travel guide books by Travel Guide Publishers on your trip to different countries and places around the globe, enjoy!!!

Printed in Great Britain
by Amazon

35180219R00116